“Thoughts” of “Another” Explained

New Paradigms for the Gold Market

By James Roth

ISBN 978-1-935910-06-0

TABLE OF CONTENTS

Preface

What follows are extracts from emailings made to a gold forum in the late 1990s. The emails were compiled into longer documents sent out to Listserv subscribers.

The author was anonymous and judging by his use of the language, a foreigner. His ideas so roiled the gold community that they have been preserved in cyberspace to this day.

On the simplest level, *Another* challenged gold bugs in the way they thought about gold, gold markets, and value. Much of the thinking he tried to change is still entrenched in among precious metals buyers. This book hopes to reach those "holdouts."

On a more complex level, *Another* gave the community paradigms to understand a framework for understanding gold price suppression. These are powerful: the oil-gold-dollar nexus; gold going where it needs to flow; the long-term accumulation at bargain rates by "giants;" and the now popular meme of gold flowing irreversibly from West to East.

Please see the Afterword in this book for a full discussion of *Another*, his ideas, influence, and context.

The conventions in transcribing *Another's* writing are as follows:

- Punctuation has been tidied up only to a point
- No text has been cut without ellipses being added [...]
- No syntax has been altered
- Misspellings have been corrected
- Needed capitalization appears in brackets [X]

All this is to say that every attempt has been made to preserve the style and flavor of the author's communications.

We have added a substantial Afterword to this volume in order not to get between the reader and *Another*. We wish for the reader to dive in without major forewords, notes, commentary, or other distractions.

Foreword

This book if for you if you believe ...

- The gold price is suppressed
- The gold markets make no sense
- Gold is money
- Currency is not money

This book is also for you if you imagine ...

- The right gold trade can make you rich
- Success is a matter of timing
- Mining stocks are a good buy
- Gold is in a bubble
- You need to diversify your portfolio
- Silver is as good as gold

The editor of this compilation became interested in gold before that fateful day of August 15, 1971. He noticed even in those days that the gold community was dominated by a trading mentality with lots of gold bugs waiting for a future payoff in fiat.

He noticed that gold buyers valued everything in the despised U.S. dollar.

He despaired of the time horizons, impatience, confusion, and naiveté.

The anonymous writer called "*Another*" was also so disturbed by what he saw in the U.S. gold community that he risked breaking his cover as a confidential advisor to major traders.

He did this to straighten us out.

These are some of his "Thoughts."

I will write here. Our Thoughts belong to the world.

Another, November 21, 1997

1. Money vs. Currency

"Gold is the only money the world has ever known" Sounds like a simple thought but it isn't.

"Money is whatever people say it is" - Not true!

"Currency is whatever a government says it is" - True!

Another, October 09, 1997

What is money? We gold fans have always said, a medium of exchange and a store of value. If something is not doing both, it is not money.

Currency is a medium of exchange created by the government. It can be paper, with no intrinsic value; it can be coins with junk metal value; it can be precious metal, which would make it currency and money both.

Previously, half a cent worth of copper stamped by the U.S. Mint would represent one cent of money. Today, seven cents worth of copper stamped by the U.S. Mint is worth one cent. So...

"Currency is whatever a government says it is" - True!

As I write, a hedge fund trader named Kyle Bass has filled a warehouse with nickels. When he placed his order, the nickel contained seven cents worth of metal content. But here is no way he can unlock that value without melting currency, which is illegal.

"Money is whatever people say it is" - Not true!

Mr. Bass may not know it, but he is testing *Another's* idea by acting as if the nickel is money.

A modern economist will say that the U.S. dollar is a *debt instrument* issued to extinguish our debts (taxes) to our government. If this is its purpose, it is not money.

One analyst compares currency to coupons saying they resemble tickets you might buy entering a carnival or fair; you use them on the fairgrounds but they do not store value.

Gold stores value and gold has been the medium of exchange.

Some time ago gold not only was used as money but also circulated as currency. It had always been money and people had no use for a separate currency to represent "gold money" so they stamped the gold itself and used it as circulating currency.

Another, October 09, 1997

This is another way to say that some time ago the currency or medium of exchange (the thaler, real, denarius, bezant, etc.) was not separate from the store of value (precious metal).

Any discovery of gold or silver was a discovery of money. You took your ore to the refinery and then to the mint where it was stamped into coin. Discovered gold or silver was found money.

In more recent times, gold stored in banks or vaults was represented by receipts. The receipts could be traded as if representing the gold. Eventually governments issued paper currency redeemable in precious metal. Look around a coin shop and you will see some dollar bills that look like today's currency except for the marking "silver certificate." The U.S. has been on both gold and silver standards.

Until August 15, 1971, dollars were redeemable by gold (on a nation-to-nation basis). All foreign currencies were pegged to the dollar, and thereby, gold. After August 15, 1971, the value of currencies "floated" against each other without reference to gold.

Today, currencies represent nothing more than the "full faith and credit" of government, its ability to tax, borrow, and issue more currency.

The "full faith and credit" backing means only that *a dollar will represent a dollar and be honored as a dollar* whatever a "dollar" (or franc or peso) will mean in the near future.

This is what separates the store of value from currency. Gold will have value, currency will remain an accounting unit.

When gold was the accounting unit, it could circulate providing both functions, store of value and accounting unit.

The western world today, as we know it does not use money! They use "paper currency". To fully understand what that really means you must come to terms with this fact. "When you use paper currency you are placing a value using another person's concept of value." You are using a thought as a means of value!

Another, October 09, 1997

After August 15, 1971, when currencies began to "float" against each other, they were priced against each other and especially against the dollar. The values fluctuated in trading venues based on the opinions (thoughts) of the traders.

In some countries, there is no float. The government sets the exchange value of the currency. The people who live in such places think hard about whether they will accept the government's currency in exchange for goods and services. Sometimes they barter instead or they may collect foreign currency such as dollars to use in daily transactions. The value of their currency is also a thought—their government's idea.

Where currencies are freely traded, the thoughts of the buyers and sellers of that market, that day, determine the value of the currency.

In the U.S., the Federal Reserve adjusts the cost of dollars by adjusting interest rates. The rates the government pays bondholders makes dollars more or less attractive because dollars are needed to buy Treasury securities that earn interest. The Federal Reserve has a thought, a concept of dollar value and wants us to have the same opinion.

The important point about using "thought as a means of value" is the frequency and scope at which thoughts change.

The Pennsylvania farmer in 1863 does not want Confederate currency for his cattle - it rates low in his thoughts. Today's African, buying American grain will pay more or less today based on "thoughts" in grain markets which value grain in currency. The American, buying a foreign car, will pay an amount based on the ideas formed by currency market participants.

At the point of exchange, someone else's concept of value completes your transaction.

... how can paper currency that represents "the thoughts of a nation blowing in the wind" be used to value real money of ancient world class proportions, gold? It cannot! Any price you can think of will do, as in *no price will work*!

Another, October 09, 1997

Today, gold is traded in markets using currency and since August 15, 1971, currency values represent "the thoughts of a nation blowing in the wind."

In other words, today we price gold using free-floating currency. This is backwards. Logically, gold prices currency. It prices everything.

If gold is a store of value, that value is not dollars (or pounds or lira), it is gold. When *Another* says "No price will work," he means that the value of gold cannot be expressed in currency units which are thoughts blowing in the wind.

The market value of gold today is the price in currency that some gold owners will accept for units of gold. This does not express the value of gold; it expresses a transaction record.

Market transactions are not value statements, although public gold owners like central banks may use market transactions to try to value their gold holdings in national currency units.

A second aspect of *Another's* statement deals in time.

The value of the currency we are using to buy gold was set in currency markets yesterday or today and will change tomorrow. The value of the gold we are buying spans epochs from the "ancient world" until now.

Depending on circumstances, the ancient trader might get one or two shovels for his bullion coin but the coin is not priced in shovels!

By the same token, our gold is not priced in fiat.

From the day of our birth we are taught to value all things using the one factor alone, currency!

Another, May 26, 1998

We share a crippling mental block in thinking about exchange and value.

Imagine, from birth, being taught to value all things using one factor alone, gold. The gold would not *have* value, the gold would *be* value. The price of a house, for instance, would be in units of gold.

Today, the price of the house is in dollars. We do not ask the price of the dollar in houses, or in fractions of a house, nor the price of the dollar in anything else. The dollar is the "value."

This is crazy because the dollar is a *thought blowing in the wind*. If the dollar (or any fiat) has a bad day on the currency markets, the cost of everything may change. It will take more (or fewer) dollars to buy bread not because the bread supply went up or down but because the unit of accounting changed value overnight.

We are using an accounting measure that changes every day. Imagine a ruler changing scale every day.

Think of it this way: this morning, you bought bread using today's dollars. Tomorrow's dollars are going to be different. Your loaf may have less weight. Have you noticed that a pound of coffee is not 16 ounces? That a pint glass does not hold a pint of beer? One way of coping with the changing value of fiat is to alter the volume of product sold.

We are taught to value everything in fiat and so we think that it is not the dollar that is changing, it is the coffee, or beer, or bread. The manufacturer is playing tricks. Or perhaps there is a shortage somewhere that is passed on to us.

Valuing things in currency hurts our ability to talk intelligently about prices, value, and exchange.

Understand, all value judgments today are as subject to "exchange rate competition"!

Another, May 26, 1998

We live in a thought prison where we have to value things in unstable national currencies. These currencies, where traded freely, embody "thoughts blowing in the wind" because currency values are set in currency markets by random notions (sentiments, opinions, hopes, fears).

Whatever the ideas of today's traders, the wind blowing through also includes puffs of *exchange rate competition*. Governments intervene in currency markets to strengthen, weaken, or stabilize the cost of their currency against the price of other currencies.

As I write this, the U.S. government faces a dilemma.

On the one hand, a highly valued dollar will allow it to borrow more money from foreigners.

On the other hand, a weak dollar will make U.S. produced goods and services cheaper abroad. This will act like a price discount in foreign markets. This will promote exports and earn more income for exporters. It will help the manufacturing economy.

The government will decide on a (temporary) policy that makes the dollar strong or weak. It will act in currency markets against other currencies.

These are some of the considerations in national exchange rate competition. It is a contest in which states intervene in markets to produce outcomes that suit their *temporary policies*.

This is a second layer of value judgments destabilizing the value of our so-called money.

Again, I ask, how can we know a true value for our assets, when they are known only in currency that finds its worth as in the exchange rate for another currency?

Another, May 26, 1998

If currency can only be valued against some other currency which is valued against yet other currencies, then we have entered a carnival fun house in which the exit is hard to find.

This is especially hard because in our thought prison, we value things in currency rather than valuing currency in things.

In other words, we value the real by means of the notional.

This insanity hits home in the W.C. Fields movie, *The Bank Dick*, where a bank security guard saves his firm from ruin (a real service) and is given a word of thanks and a "hearty handshake" (a notional reward).

We all have real assets. We own real things. But the system for valuing our reality is to apply currency units, in other words hearty handshakes, the worth of which are based on the exchange rates for other currencies which represent *thoughts blowing in the wind as well as exchange rate competition by governments*.

The true value of our assets cannot be expressed in fiat currency. The most fiat currency can do for us is to express a temporary and unstable exchange value between today's fiat and the valued asset.

The "game of currencies has not ended" and has produced "asset valuations" that would not exist if converted into real things. As such, the wealth of nations that many believe they hold does not exist today, in dollar terms, nor will it exist tomorrow!

Another, June 29, 1998

To understand the value of our various assets, we apply currency units which are valued against other currency units.

Currency values circle each other in a witches' brew stirred by national policy and *thoughts in the wind*. From this we derive ideas of value for real assets. But these statements of value are notional based on the swirl of currency exchanges and "the game of currencies" that governments play.

Consider that "the wealth of nations" might include natural resources, reserves of foreign currencies, bonds, land, and various forms of private wealth. Aside from being valued based on "thoughts in the wind," all of these things are certainly mispriced due to the governments' intentional *game of currencies*.

If assets were valued against assets, some assets might be revealed to have no value at all. This is the wealth that does not exist but is carried on the books.

On a personal level, we have all heard stories of the type that "a cup of coffee used to cost 10 cents." The idea behind these stories is not that a cup of coffee is so much more valuable today but that coffee today is *totally mispriced in currency terms*.

Whomever is telling you these stories gets that. If you have stored up enough beans for 100 cups of coffee is your wealth worth $10 (per old prices) or $100 (per new prices)?

The wealth of nations could best be expressed by the value of real things measured against real things. To measure the worth of real things in currency terms is an exercise in self-deception.

A currency loses value because persons do not want to use it for commerce or savings.

Another, September 3, 1998

We have seen the old photographs of Germans lighting stoves using paper currency.

Currency is an accounting unit whose value is set by thoughts in the wind. It can stop being useful as an accounting unit.

We all know the ways:

- The supply is too much or too little or fluctuates to much
- Rumors say something will happen to the currency
- The government issuing the currency is in trouble
- A better alternative is easier to use or more attractive or more accessible.

If people have been using currency to try to store value, they give it up when:

- It depreciates
- A change is rumored or announced
- The government issuing the currency is in trouble
- Fewer people want it and will do business with it

The government can try different things to force people to use its currency but if people at home do not want to use it, it will lose ground on foreign exchanges as well.

The change in sentiment seems to come quickly, if history is a guide.

Rich in paper until the world says, "this paper, it is not good"!

Another, May 5, 1998

The central banks of the world are rich in paper, their own and the paper of other states. Private fortunes currently rest in stocks, bonds, derivatives, cash. The paper rich will remain rich in that way until sentiment changes.

We see in history that the world is quick to say "this paper, it is not good" when the time comes. Sentiment changes in a rush.

In the U.S. the dollar is a debt obligation, a bond issued by the Treasury worth one dollar. It is a debt certificate. The day may come when we ask:

"How many debt certificates do I need to buy 10 gallons of gasoline?"

"What will you give me for 100 debt certificates?"

Argentina went through a period of "dollarization" when their people decided the peso was no good. When the U.S. debt certificates are no longer wanted, with what can the USA be dollarized?

A man (or a business or a government) could accumulate paper. He would fool himself to think that he had accumulated the value of a factory or oil well or farm by holding the equivalent notional value in paper money. But the value of the paper is outside of his control.

The value of the real thing, however, is the value of the real thing.

The rich man can be rich in paper one day and then quickly ruined by the world saying his currency (or other paper) is no good. It is important not to be "rich in paper" for this reason.

This is also why many warn against holding paper claims to gold or gold equivalents.

We have all seen Confederate currency, Zimbabwean billion dollar notes, and stock and bond certificates from vanished firms.

From the start, one thing most thinkers can't quite grasp is that "money does not have to circulate!" The first "world money," gold money that is, could stay locked up and still represent value and wealth.

Another, October 9, 1997

Modern economists think of money mainly as currency rather than as a "store of value". They see a social and economic benefit in the "velocity of money."

You bought this book for 10 units of currency. I bought a chicken from you for 10 units of currency. You bought another book for 10 units of currency. I bought another chicken from you. And so on. Ten units of currency might move through the economy as 40 (+) units spent. This is seen as stimulating prosperity under current thinking.

The choice I might make after the first exchange, to store my 10 units and not spend it, economists view as a bad thing. My 10 units are transformed into a different function in the economy. They represent stored wealth.

Modern economists are unfamiliar with the effects of stored wealth and with its implications.

The job of an accounting unit is to enable exchange. If currency is an accounting unit, the economist thinks it is not doing that job sitting in a safe. It stops being money if it sits still.

At the same time, we know it cannot safely store value because it is an accounting unit valued against other accounting units in the battle of the exchange rates and under continuous state intervention.

If we think about what *Another* says here, he seems to be giving more weight to money's "store of value" function than its function as a "medium of exchange."

Another has asked us to imagine money as both a medium of exchange and a store of value. We should also ponder which one of those functions is more important than the other.

One of the great money troubles facing the western currency system today is that many third world people are starting to put a "mind value" on real money, gold. These people don't know the true value of gold money but they know it's worth a whole lot more than the world paper currency price now placed on it.

Another, October 9, 1997

We don't know who *Another* was but he is believed to have been an Asian active in gold markets and this observation represents a theme with him.

The currencies of the world misprice everything, including gold. So we see a system of "premiums" which are used to adjust the local gold price (against currency) in different markets. These premiums vary widely especially country-to-country.

It's interesting that the western gold buyer uses the prices of currency and paper gold as benchmarks and the eastern buyer does not.

Additionally, *Another* indicated something that has gained wider acceptance in our day, namely that large transactions are managed off the books at huge premiums over the spot price of gold.

In the third world, private people are taking the "store of value" part of money, detaching it from the idea of currency, and acting on that. The "mind value" of gold is the price people are willing to pay in currency for locally available gold irrespective of the international market values.

If the "mind value" ignores the currency-based pricing of gold, then available gold will move out of the West and into the Third World, where it will "disappear" into private holdings.

This trend had begun when *Another* began writing and it has now become a common topic among alternative investors. The gold flow is West to East, thanks to this "mind power."

The best way to rework the public's mind about gold money was by changing the way it was viewed. "It's money of course but let's also call it a 'commodity!' Then we can place a 'paper' value on it and denominate it in all forms of future contracts. It will lose its true value as money in peoples' minds and be priced in an unrealistic paper format." And here we are today!

Another, October 9, 1997

In recent historical times, the times of our grandparents in many cases, money was valued against gold or silver or both.

This is very hard for a modern person to understand or digest: *the currency had no intrinsic value except as expressed against gold.*

Gold was gold. Ten dollars could express a certain weight in gold. No gold, no value for the $10. Today, our thinking is reversed. Gold has no value except as expressed in currency.

But if gold is a commodity like wheat, soybeans, or oil, we can trade contracts for dollars on the exchanges and the gold's "value" in dollars will be the value of those contracts, those trades.

Today, gold is NOT priced based on physical gold sales. Goldprice.org explains that on the Commodities Exchange (COMEX) "The real-time, second by second, spot price of gold is the price of the futures contract of the 'most active month' as it is trading on the exchange." This is the famous "spot price" that is used to value gold in currency. It derives from futures contracts.

The gold contracts trading on exchanges is many time larger than the world's gold supply. There is not a one-to-one match, by any means.

Thus, Gold's value in the West is a little like a thought blowing on the wind showing an "unrealistic" price in currencies.

Its "mindshare" regresses to paper in the West, where the exchanges are and where the modern concept of money-as-currency holds sway.

Today, all modern money does have "reserves," and such is used only for "the dirty float" in currency warfare.

Another, May 21, 1998

In olden times, the currency was minted gold. Later, paper represented gold. The paper was currency, the gold was used as reserves. Paper could act as money because the gold it represented was a store of value.

Today, the central banks that issue currency hold reserves in other currencies. (They also hold some gold but the gold is or was a small fraction of the reserves.)

In the past, the reserves (silver or gold) backed the currency. Today, the reserve serves other purposes. It is commonly used to interfere with currency markets. The intention can be helpful (to stabilize a currency's value) or harmful (to drive a competitor's currency values up or down).

James Rickards famously writes about "currency warfare," buying or selling to improve the position of the dollar (for instance) or hurt the position of a competing currency.

From Wikipedia:

> Managed float regime is the current international financial environment in which exchange rates fluctuate from day to day, but central banks attempt to influence their countries' exchange rates by buying and selling currencies. It is also known as a dirty float.

"Managed" is a nicer word than "dirty" and "influence" is nicer than "warfare." (If central banks were out of currency markets , that would be a "clean float.")

Without foreign currency reserves, nations cannot operate the dirty float.

Another has exposed the modern use for "reserves." These are not your grandfather's central bank reserves.

In [the] "cold war" of modern exchange rates, "digital currencies from reserves are used," however, when "hot war" of major default does begin, "nuclear weapons of GOLD" are deployed!

Another, May 21, 1998

Only a fraction of the central bank's reserves are held in gold. Any central bank's gold operations are very mysterious and therefore best addressed by careful speculation.

Now, as *Another* suggests, there was and is a currency war in which states try to position the value of their currencies in that "cold war," using their reserves to "dirty the float." As this is written, Japan is going all out to cheapen its own currency, the yen, in order to make its exports more attractive.

Another pictures an event, a default, triggering an end to the currency war. In our day such an event might involve the USA not paying interest on its debt or repudiating part or all of its Treasury bills, notes, or bonds. This action would be so drastic as to collapse the value of dollars held abroad.

The most devastating retaliation against a default would be for a government to link its currency to gold on a fractional value basis. (This would not require a lot of gold.) The perpetrator would become "king of the currencies" overnight with everyone dumping paper money to get into the gold-backed money. This nuke would win the currency war by destroying the value of all competitors at a stroke. It would force exports and imports to be valued in the new currency.

The outcome would be so devastating as to deserve *Another's* term "nuclear weapon."

This, as we shall see, appears to be what *Another* envisioned as a "hot," "nuclear" currency war.

All nations will use the same digital currencies for all trade, but will also add gold to the value. The world will not end, it will change

Another, January 11, 1998

Another wrote this six months before the formal establishment of the European Central Bank (ECB). As the bank was being organized, it was decided that it would have a fixed amount of reserves and that a fixed amount of gold would make up part of its reserves.

It was also decided that the value of its gold holdings would be "marked to market," that is constantly revalued at market prices. The result has been that the value of the ECB's reserves has been going up as the price of gold has gone up.

Gold has not been used to back the Euro currency but it does improve the solvency of the central bank issuing the currency. In that indirect way, gold has been added to the value and a major change has happened.

Meanwhile, as of June 30, 2013, the U.S. Treasury says it holds 258,641,878 troy ounces of gold valued at $10.92 billion: about $42 an ounce. This is the government's own fixed price for gold. The spot price values gold at $1,377 an ounce as this is written. Unlike the ECB, the U.S. Treasury's gold is not adding value to the reserves.

Another is also suggesting that multi-currency settlements can work if there is an underlying gold component. Nowadays we hear talk of creating a trade settlement "basket of currencies" that includes gold.

There has also been an explosion in experimental bilateral exchanges bypassing dollar settlements. Iran is under an embargo and Turkey has been acting as a gold settlement and clearing house for Iranian gold-backed trade..

We are very close to seeing *Another's* prediction come true. The devil is in the details but the details are being worked out in practice.

As some say "not enough gold to use as a currency", I say "gold not valued high enough to use as currency." At a high enough value (price) it is an excellent currency!

Another, January 11, 1998

This is to say that at higher gold values, less gold is needed to back money in circulation. Small national holdings can back large currency supplies at a high enough price.

What *Another* was countering here was those who say that the massive number of currency units circulating in a large economy would so fragment a central bank's gold supply as to make but tiny gold grains the backing of this or that unit of currency ... and *that* would be and restrictive and impractical.

Some goldbugs today counter that tiny bits backing currency units would be perfectly okay.

Consider this: If gold is mispriced by being marked to the currency markets and paper contracts, then it should not be used to back currency on the basis of current fantasy pricing. (At the time *Another* wrote this thought, gold was priced in the hundreds of dollars.)

Another suggests that when markets can discover the real price of gold, the holding of central banks would be more than adequate for currency backing. A higher value would also increase the value of the currency backed by gold.

An "excellent currency" would be a more useful currency and a currency that is worth more per unit.

2. The Dollar and Fiat

At present, I, like you, must view the world thru dollar. The "world reserve trading currency" it remains!

Another, August 11, 1998

No matter how strong gold may be in reality or potentially, international trade is settled in dollars. Mentally we translate bid and offer into dollars. We "value" goods in dollar terms, as strange as this is.

When American President Richard Nixon stopped the exchange of gold for dollars in U.S .foreign trade, the dollar without gold backing replaced the dollar that had been backed by gold. A kind of shadow dollar carried on in trade settlement.

In those days "strong" dollar policies were popular political policies and dollar holders abroad were less concerned about the dollar losing value against other currencies.

America also succeeded in having Saudi Arabia settle oil trades in dollars. This had a domino effect. The industrialized world needs oil for everything and today it needs dollars to pay for oil.

The biggest move away from the dollar was the creation of the Euro, which allowed intra-European trade without resort to dollars. The next biggest move will come when oil trades are settled in other currencies or in gold.

In the meantime, the dollar has "mind share" in valuing all kinds of transactions in currencies, commodities, imports, realty, and so on.

The tragedy in this is that the dollar's own value is a thought blowing in the wind.

Today, all currencies are traded against the dollar for its usage as a medium of oil exchange! Take away that link and the entire currency/ debt exchange system, as we know it will collapse!

Another, November 2, 1997

The dollar's status as a world reserve currency is due mainly because almost all oil trades must be settled in dollars. ("Almost" because some states are starting to leave dollar settlement to make direct exchanges in their own currencies.)

All countries need oil which means all countries need dollars to buy oil. In this sense, the dollar is oil backed.

Countries collect dollars in their central banks; dollars are earned through trade, or they are borrowed, or they are bought at prevailing exchange rate. Dollars are also earned in the form of dollar interest on dollar debt instruments, like U.S. Treasury bills, bonds, and notes.

Central banks and other holders of dollars (foreign commercial banks, foreign businesses, and wealthy individuals) don't want their cash dollars sitting idle, so they buy "safe" bonds, bills, and notes from the U.S. Treasury. These represent debt obligations of the United States.

The continuous trade in oil generates demand for dollars and dollar debt instruments. This allows the U.S. to borrow money heavily through its bonds, bills and notes. As this is written, 40% of the U.S. federal budget is borrowed by issuing Treasury instruments.

Just as our minds are trained to value real things in currency, oil is valued in the dollar. If the link were to break, it is unlikely that oil sellers would want to take some other currency in lieu of dollars. They would probably price oil in gold.

This is what *Another* means when he says breaking the link between oil and dollars will collapse the currency/debt system. More than 15 years after he wrote these words, central banks are accumulating gold. Some observers say this will play a role in future trade settlement. In that case, currency will be an accounting unit for domestic transactions.

Oil is only priced in US$ worldwide. Gold is only priced in US$ worldwide. It is important that this process of dollar backing continue, as it is the only thing keeping this "digital currency" alive!

Another, December 12, 1997

Remember that *Another* suggested exchange rates are but a transitory thought or idea and a plaything of the "dirty float."

One can say there are two tiers of currency: dollars and non-dollars.

In the lower tier, currencies are valued against each based on "ideas," central bank policies, and "thoughts in the wind." They are also, ultimately, valued against dollars.

At the dollar level, pricing is against gold and oil. The dollar sits at the nexus of gold and oil values and is used to express these (no matter how distorted those values may be).

We said there is a sense by which oil backs dollars; in the same sense gold backs dollars. It is more accurate to say, the gold and oil trade back dollars. They don't back its value, they back its use as an international medium of exchange and asset.

If oil or gold were priced differently and their trade settled outside of dollars, this "digital currency" would die.

At best, the dollar would become a domestic accounting unit used to settle debts and pay taxes in America.

Oil functions as the true gold for the modern world. Indeed, it was only when the world started needing oil for everything that gold was dropped as backing for the US$ and replaced with oil!

Another, December 12, 1997

Another here refers to President Richard Nixon closing the gold window in foreign trade settlement and then signing an agreement with King Faisal of Saudi Arabia that would settle all Saudi oil sales in dollars.

Given that oil is needed for everything, everyone needs the currency that buys oil. The skyrocketing worldwide demand for oil created a similar demand for dollars, which are needed to buy oil.

Oil functions as the "true gold" in this way: everyone needs it; economies cannot function without it.

What makes it different is that it is consumed - it does not store value. But because it is priced in dollars, dollars can be accumulated as oil equivalents.

Storing dollars stores the equivalent value (market price) of oil.

Again, without the oil connection, the countries of the world would not need to store so many dollars. They exchange their currency for dollars to make the oil trade.

Oil is "true gold" in having value, as in being central to trade, central to the economy, and central to national wealth or poverty.

The US$ must be maintained as the "most used" if the other currencies are to have a chance to survive. Will Japan sell US treasury debt and risk taking dollars out of "usage"? Not in your life!

Another, November 2, 1997

Foreign currencies measure their usefulness in terms of buying dollars (needed to buy oil and settle other trade). A strong, useful local currency buys a lot of dollars and with that a lot of oil and other goods.

Local currency is used to transact local business. It "lives" internationally only in relation to the dollar-gold-oil nexus. Its gateway to the nexus is the USD.

The more the dollar is used internationally, the better the survival rate for currencies that are directly or indirectly priced against the dollar and used to buy dollars for trade settlement.

If dollars become undesirable, the oil trade (and other trade) becomes more expensive, harder to conduct, and every local currency would suffer its own "desirability crisis" as everything would have to be repriced in local currency instead of dollars.

The demand for baht in Mexico and pesos in Thailand would shape Thai-Mexican trade.

In the oil trade, it seems that local currencies, where used to buy oil, would naturally be discounted by the oil buyers based on the desirability of their currency.

Since the dollar backs all currencies worldwide as a "reserve," if the dollar weakens or is shunned, the national reserves are weakened with an indirect effect on the national currency.

Since this thought was written, the Euro has emerged as alternate medium of trade exchange and as a reserve currency. This alters the dynamic somewhat.

Nations will defend the system at all cost. They will never sell US$ Treasury debt as that debt is their currency!

Another, November 7, 1997

This is a concise way of saying that central bank reserves back the local currency and those reserves are USD instruments: notes, bills and bonds. Thus, the local currency is backed by central bank holdings of dollars.

But *Another* uses the term "nations" which implies more than the central bank.

Indeed, businesses everywhere have treasury departments that manage their foreign exchange activities. Businesses buy and sell dollars and dollar instruments. They are part of this dollar system as well. They typically use Treasury debt to store their excess dollars.

Dollars are the basis of the current international monetary system. Take away the dollars and there is no system.

Indeed, all other currencies have reserves of US$ to back them, yet only the dollar has nothing!

Another, April 25, 1998

Central banks hold foreign currency reserves, mainly dollars in the form of U.S. Treasury debt. That and the power of taxation backs their currencies.

The USD does not derive its backing from America's foreign currency reserves. In fact, the USA's foreign currency reserves are valued in dollar terms!

The dollar, has nothing behind it except "full faith and credit" plus market mandates to settle gold and oil trades in dollars.

When *Another* wrote this, central banks were selling gold. Now they are buying it for their reserves. Perhaps a change is coming.

In our present system, all currencies are backed by the US$. As long as the US$ is on an "oil standard" of backing, no other country can change.

Another, January 23, 1998

Previously, *Another* said that the dollar has no backing. Here, he refers to an oil standard.

Here is the distinction. Dollars are the unit of measurement, the standard, for oil trading. They are the sole unit of account for oil transactions.

The dollar is not backed by oil, per se, it is made useful by its role in the oil trade.

This is the core point: that there is a chain of value.

Oil > dollar > foreign currencies

Currency can play a role locally but not internationally, except to buy dollars that are needed to buy oil.

Another refers to the "present system" but now, 15 years later, we see central banks preparing for a "future system" by stockpiling gold. Meanwhile, trade ministries start to make bilateral deals to exchange local currency for oil.

Countries seem to be planning for a future change, one that was impossible to conceive of until now.

If US$ is reserve for all other currencies, how can other currencies be held as reserve for US$?

Another, April 26, 1998

The BIS does not recognize other currencies as reserves, as they are, in themselves, a dollar product!

Another, April 26, 1998

Set aside the question of the Euro for a moment.

When this was written, the USD had been the agreed upon currency for the settlement of trade per the Bretton Woods agreement.

By the 1990s, for trade purposes, the use of foreign currencies was in the purchase of dollars. A strong foreign currency bought more dollars. With this in mind, it makes no sense to say that the foreign currency holdings of United States constitute a reserve.

Foreign currencies are local scrip convertible into dollars for foreign trade purposes.

Since the Euro emerged some of this has changed. But the striking thing about the Euro is its dominant function in trade settlement within the European Union.

In last resort, the dollar, it can buy "oil" or "gold" anywhere in world. In the real world, this is the "real backing" behind the dollar held in many lands!

Another, June 14, 1998

We want to square the idea of "no backing" for the dollar with this "real backing" idea.

Another is making his point through a paradox. The dollar is getting "real backing" through its acceptance in trade. That is actually a virtual backing based on goodwill ("goodwill" in the strictest business sense of the term). Today, I accept your dollars for gold. Tomorrow I may not. That is hardly backing!

And yet it has an effect as powerful as if dollars had "real backing." We might say that for the dollar, this is as "real" as it gets.

This kind of backing is based on thought or opinion as much as the price that is set on the currency exchanges.

We have pricing based on an opinion, we have acceptance based on opinion. Acceptance is "more real" than dollar pricing because it is tied to oil and gold.

It can go from "real backing" to "no backing" as quickly as any thoughts blowing in the wind.

... "a currency unit exists only during the moment of trade." During this time, when real things are in transit, paper currency has value as an expected "trade completion." It exists as a human thought. Complete the transaction and the thought is gone, the currency unit dies.

Another, January 17, 1998

The currency is of but momentary value expressed as "the intention of a trade completion." Complete the trade and "poof" the units hold no future value.

Another, February 7, 1998

Currency's value "comes alive" for the briefest moment at the point of exchange where it is traded for something tangible or for services.

The currency I pay for beets completes the trade and extinguishes my desire for beets at that moment. It may or may not buy the same number or quality of beets at the next trade.

The paper accounting unit that paid for beets - dollars or pesos, whatever - lives on in someone's pocket after the exchange as an abstract accounting unit. It will complete more trades as human thought arises, thought that matches the available unit against the desire for some value.

The value is outside the currency unit.

At each trade, the value of the exchange will be expressed in currency units, whereas the real value resides in the thing bought with currency units.

The buyer and seller will turn in for a night's rest while currency markets worldwide reset the buying power of the currency units in their wallets based on sentiment, opinion, demand, supply, and many and various ideas.

It is the value of the currency unit that dies after the exchange. It will be reborn endlessly and on scales driven by human thought.

Without trade, modern currencies have no use, no value, no purpose.

Another, January 17, 1998

"Real value is not needed for modern money, as it is only used as a trading unit!"

Another, January 17, 1998

Today, digital currencies are not to hold value, but to use for trade only.

Another, April 18, 1998

This modern paper is but a "receipt in commerce!" If a person holds a "paper trade receipt" as a savings for life, how can wealth be gained?

Another, April 18, 1998

Try to picture currency as being useful outside of commercial exchange. Its only function would be in paying taxes, since the government issues its own currency and accepts payment in same.

Paper money does not store value: its uses are limited to transactions.

Governments and people do stockpile currencies but they convert them to treasury bills, notes and bonds so as to earn interest. The currency itself is traded for government paper.

Any mark-to-market valuation of stored currency ("paper trade receipt") is an accounting procedure and hypothetical, subject to changing ideas and opinions.

The stored currency unit (a trade receipt) takes on value in some future trade, but that value cannot be predicted. Wealth cannot be secured by collecting paper of unknown future value.

A dead yen be a dead Japan.

Another, May 5, 1998

All economies today are truly equal in production as the exchange rates are the manufactures of profit!"

Another, May 5, 1998

Another once proposed that if the Bank of Japan (BoJ) sold off its U.S. treasuries, if it hurt the dollar, that would kill the yen because the yen (like all currencies) is a derivative of the USD.

Today, we see the the BoJ driving the yen value down through money printing. This will cause exports to be cheaper. Now Japan risks killing the yen in a different way: to sell more exports. You might say that the government thinks the yen must die in order for Japan to live.

But this is a mistake as well.

First, it will take more yen to buy dollars for Japan's imports. It will gain more on exports and lose it in imports. Oil becomes more expensive. Savings are expropriated.

Second, this is action is aggressive currency warfare. As Jim Rickards notes, no currency war has yielded a victor and all have ended in ruin.

There may be different ways to produce dead yen but the outcome will be the same.

Meanwhile, through stock market reports, investors are learning quarter by quarter that much of their company's profit was gained by a favorable exchange rate during the reporting period.

A second way to say what *Another* states is this: that the quantity and quality of national production are less important than the exchange rates that inflate or depress the earnings of that production.

Japan knows this. Other governments know this which is why they wage a continuous "exchange rate war" against each other. They seek maximum trade advantage through currency manipulation.

Yes, there is supply of the currency, and we have demand for the currency, but the end product is as the space between stars!

Another, February 7, 1998

"The space between the stars" is the void of a completed transaction. The currency fulfilled its duty when it enabled a transaction.

The currency was in demand to complete transactions. Currency is bought and sold and earned and invested - these are transactions that enable other transactions.

At the center of this activity is the void of value that can be stored.

All modern digital currencies do not go into an investment, they move THRU it.

Another, January 23, 1998

How can one know value in currency, when paper does not lie still?

Another , February 22, 1998

No CB holds any currency! They hold the bonds of that currency.

Another, January 23, 1998

As various investment scandals and collapses show, the investor's money does not sit quietly in a safe, or even in a protected (segregated) account. The investor's money is traveling around the world in such far-away places that sometimes, it is unable to come back to its owner. It does not lie still.

Think about personal banking. Once the deposit is made, the bank owns the money and the depositor owns a receipt for the money. Money we deposit with the bank is put to other uses.

Investment money stays even busier.

The purchase of an investment gives us the right to a future transaction of unknown value. If we own a share of stock we own the right to sell a share. The money used to buy the stock does not reside in the stock. Its "price" or "value" is nothing more than the latest record of someone else's buying or selling.

Neither does currency lie still unless hoarded by its owner. Even the Central Banks exchange their currency for government bills, notes and bonds that represent a promise for future payments. They "own" dollars through the Treasuries they accumulate. But the dollars they paid for their Treasuries have moved on.

Currency has moved *through* their investments and is traveling elsewhere.

There is a funny new financial word that describes one of the crooked paths taken by money on the move: "rehypothecation."

Are the bullion banks bonded? In the real national/ world there is no such thing as "bonded".

Another, February 4, 1998

As this is written, there are six large bullion banks operating in the world. These are banks that take gold deposits, lease gold, and perform other gold transactions, mainly for central banks.

The holdings of the bullion banks are in no sense "guaranteed" to be where they are nor doing the job they are supposed to do.

The owner of a gold deposit, for instance, has a piece of paper entitling the return of that gold, but the gold itself might be leased out, sold short into the market, encumbered by the bank's derivative operations or otherwise manipulated.

The gold in a bullion bank does not lie still. That bank is not a warehouse and its contents are not bonded.

There are only two threats to the world fiat currency system at present. The oil states could stop buying US$ for oil and drop all paper gold for real bullion. Or, the masses could buy up all the physical supplies thereby breaking the OIL/GOLD/US$ bond.

Another, December 12, 1997

If the oil states switched from dollars to Euros or Yuan in settling trades, the world's fiat money system would continue. However, if gold were used to settle oil trades, the fiat system would lose its usefulness.

You might split the difference, however. Imagine that gold and dollars *both* are needed to settle oil trades - this would at least undermine the world's paper currency system, though not destroy it.

Another said that in his time, some settlement was being done in dollars in combination with call options on gold.

The call options on gold would have been a hedge the dollar suddenly declining. Gold is priced in dollars and would be expected to rise if the dollar was falling. So, if the U.S. began printing dollars, the gold call option's value would move "into the money" allowing the oil seller to cash it out, getting more dollars (or gold).

On the other hand, if the oil states demanded a 100% gold payment, oil would be priced in gold and gold would be priced in oil. The value of the dollar would sink and no central bank would need to hold dollars, thus unleashing a tidal wave of dollars returning from overseas and with it massive U.S. inflation. "The world fiat currency system" would become a "local fiat currency system" as fiat could only serve a local purpose: taxes and local commerce.

Another mentions a second scenario: physical gold shortage caused by retail demand. Currently, in gold circles a favorite "what if" scenario imagines that the general public in the West suddenly takes an interest in gold and begins buying. The point here is the tiny amount of gold currently in private hands and the stress on the gold system that retail buying would cause.

When (through scarcity or market trauma) neither gold nor oil can be priced in dollars, the link is broken and fiat crashes.

If a crisis erupts and gold breaks the bond with oil, then a change must take place!

Another, January 23, 1998

Should the price of gold in dollars skyrocket, the oil seller will not want dollars.

Dollars being the bridge between oil and gold prices, a substitute would have to be found or else gold and oil would have to be priced against each other in some other way.

Pricing oil in gold might actually be a first step towards pricing everything in gold.

Meanwhile, any steep decline in the dollar/gold price would make the dollar less and less useful in pricing gold and oil.

Finally, consider also that a shortage of oil would have the same effect as a shortage of gold. Its price in dollars might be so high that the use of the dollar to price it becomes impractical.

This is what is meant by "a change must come."

Quiet minds will think: "I did not know dollar assets would find such a fate" and "had I known physical gold could hold such wealth, no other investment was needed!"

Another, July 19, 1998

The change that would follow a break-up of the dollar-gold-oil link might not be repaired by placing some other fiat currency in the dollar's place.

The change that would follow breakage of the dollar-gold-oil link would affect all assets denominated in fiat.

The less vulnerable assets would be tangible.

The more vulnerable assets would be intangible: stocks, CDs, bonds: paper of all kind.

If dollar assets have to be repriced in gold or oil, our minds (trained to price value in dollars) will be extremely confused and distressed.

Quiet minds may still be able to reflect on where value has resided all along.

Please understand, that wealth will move into all forms of real assets as the destruction of our debt/ digital currency system continues. When the currencies move to a final resolution, it will be the "marketplace for precious metals" that will die first!

Another, February 4, 1998

Markets need sellers as well as buyers, and if everyone is bidding and no one is asking, then the market will freeze.

This is not a permanent state but it will be the state of the market during the "final resolution" of any fiat crisis. Buyers will overmatch sellers and unlike stock exchanges, where a market maker may buy or sell just to keep the market liquid, there will be no market maker to bridge the ever wider gaps between bid and ask for precious metals.

So the marketplace for precious metals dies first, followed by the next most attractive markets.

As this is written, the U.S. Federal Reserve is pushing $85 billion a month into circulation and the money is moving "into all forms of real assets" as the dollar's value is destroyed.

Who can know the minds of men and countries as paper burns?

Another, January 23, 1998

There is a certain kind of gold advocate who lives for trading scenarios in which holdings of gold are traded for vast quantities of fiat thus scoring big paper "profits."

Even today, people will buy gold as a means to get back into paper "after the crisis."

Another has tried to correct this thinking. He says gold and precious metal markets will "die" during the crisis. That means there will be no venue in which to "score big" collecting fiat for gold.

Here he says - more generally - it is not going to be possible to game *any kind of outcomes* "as paper burns."

The minds of men will be running in many crazy directions "when paper burns."

When the economy of the dollar, becomes as your "Autumn" and arrives suddenly, they will pause from this foolishness. In that time, the savings for the future of their children will be as these dried "leaves" of winter, blowing in the wind!

Another, June 29, 1998

We live in the age of the economy of the dollar. The start of the new economy will come on as quickly as summer to autumn.

Intergenerational wealth stored in paper denominated in fiat may have no more value in this future economy than dead leaves.

The change will come as a surprise. We will have great difficulty with the surprise because our minds price everything in dollars; because we are invested in paper; because markets will change or close; because paper, in different ways, times, and places "will burn."

Trust in paper will appear, in retrospect, as foolishness.

But "risk" comes not in currency inflation by price of things, but in currency destruction thru "choice of use"!

Another, February 22, 1998

In much of the gold literature since the 1970s there has been an emphasis on inflation as danger to the currency and gold as a hedge to that. Underlying this picture is the idea that as prices rise, gold can be sold for ever more fiat, thus preserving purchasing power.

We have seen here, however, that currency will not be destroyed by inflation but by choice of use. Inflation may influence that choice, but it is the choice that is decisive.

When oil producers choose to use some other means of trade settlement, there will be currency destruction.

When people choose to use all their currency to buy gold and the gold market dies for lack of selling, currency will die.

There are currencies with high inflation; the locals can adopt a different currency to conduct their business in. This is called dollarization but it could be Euro-ization or anything. The government's inflated currency lives on for transactions wih (or approved by) the government. It does not die.

If the locals' attitude toward their currency was so hostile that it could not even be used for government transactions, or if the government lacked confidence in its own currency to transact state business, it will have been destroyed by choice of use, in fact, by the choice not to use it.

3. The Dollar Burden

But, for every one that is brought low, ten others will gain from the loss of this dollar burden.

Another, April 04 1998

Today, the dollar is used to export inflation. To the counterparties holding dollars, it is a wasting asset. To those who must trade in dollars, they must lose value with each conversion of local fiat into and out of the USD.

The world is hostage to the U.S. managed dollar economy. *It is our currency but your problem*, as Nixon's Treasury Secretary John Connally once said.

The destruction of the dollar will surely harm those holdings held in dollars and the individuals and institutions that own and collect paper.

But for the mass of wage earners, who have not been able to store value, who have been subject to currency wars, exchange and interest rate manipulation, government debt, and the host of paper money abuses, the death of the dollar will spell a kind of financial liberation.

Their work will have to be exchanged for real value and they will be able to trade real value and store it.

Many teach the way of "honest dealings" and "earn your own way", then force their neighbor to accept a currency debt receipt, as payment for "real commerce goods." The world reserve currency is held by "default" not choice.

Another, April 26, 1998

The world's reserve currency is such thanks to previous agreements and oil and gold settlement rules.

The U.S. prints dollars to buy whatever its citizens want in foreign goods. Foreign producers must accept dollars in settlement for these transactions.

There is an inherent injustice in exchanging something notional - like an accounting chit (fiat money) - for something tangible or real, like land or cattle or food.

The exchange seems to void "honest dealing" and "earning your own way" by providing a lesser value for a greater value.

Because there is no other way to effect exchanges this is our default way to trade and we hold currency - by default - to be able to trade.

In this way, currency dealings make us dishonest.

In reality, when the US government needs money, it doesn't sell debt! It "TRANSFERS" the obligation of its citizens to pay future real production (taxes) as a "backing" for its newly printed currency! As this process has been going on for decades, it has built up a debt of "real production payments" that its citizens can never pay.

Another, April 25, 1998

This refers both to the way money is created in the U.S. and to the "full faith and credit" of the government backing the currency.

The issuance of a government note, bill or bond is a promise that its taxpayers will make good on interest and principle. Any Treasury instrument generates currency for the government to spend and obligations for citizens to meet.

The issuance of Treasury paper is the means by which the U.S. government creates money.

If you think of all the dollar paper in circulation around the world as being backed by citizen production, that production might have to be extended to infinity in order to cover the debt issued.

The production of this generation of citizens cannot equal the obligations issued by their government. This is why we speak of selling the next generation into debt slavery.

The dollar has consumed the wealth of all who hold assets in these terms. The American debt is evidence of this consumption. The expansion of this debt now destroys the economies of countries that use the dollar as a reserve.

Another, June 29, 1998

Those who have earned dollars by providing worth for dollars hold paper subject to burning at any major economic shift. The paper has consumed their worth and holds it unsteadily.

U.S. public debt amounts to someone holding assets in terms of dollars and a government's promise to pay in dollars. Someone has traded an enormous amount of production for an enormous amount of paper. The paper has consumed the production.

The figure of 97% is sometimes used to explain this. It is said that adjusting for inflation, the dollar has lost 97% of its value since 1913.

The expansion of public debt lowers the exchange rate of dollars as well as their stability and desirability, weakening central bank reserves. Those central banks buying these debt instruments are exchanging local real production for paper notionally issued by the U.S. Treasury without restraint. The local economy can be damaged, even destroyed, by a misallocation of local production cause by dollar requirements.

Likewise, the flood of easy dollars in the U.S. enables credit to be mispriced. Easy credit results in private buying of goods produced abroad. Real production abroad is exchanged for the notional currency flooding the U.S. credit markets.

The American accumulates real goods, the seller accumulates dollars, distorting the producer's economy and exposing it to eventual destruction.

Neither myself, or any other person should enrich their home by holding the assets that give "bondage upon future life"

Another, April 4, 1998

Since *Another* wrote this, the general public has come to understand that U.S. debt is intergenerational. We now often hear "Our children will have to pay our debts!"

Hearing this, we might assume that the children are in bondage to the government. But they are in debt to the bondholders, as are the taxpayers of many economies in this day.

And this statement does not only apply to the holders of bills, notes and bonds but to holders of currencies.

Every dollar in circulation represents a claim on future production.

Dollars and debt instruments denominated in dollars represent "bondage upon future life."

4. Price Manipulation

Every business, asset, debt, currency and army is "priced in currency terms" that reflect a "full supply of cheap oil"!

Another, March 21, 1998

The present digital money undervalues all real things in terms of "gold real money".

Another, April 18, 1998

These statements are sides of the same coin.

The world uses oil for everything and the industrialized economy cannot function without cheap oil. The pricing of oil at depressed levels is imperative lest the world economy begin moving backwards.

Oil pricing must be suppressed for the sake of the status quo (which originated in days of cheap oil).

Because oil is used in everything, undervalued oil (oil sold at suppressed prices) becomes undervalued everything.

Because oil and gold are linked to dollars through the current settlement systems, the low price of oil has to be so reflected in gold's pricing. The relationship between gold, oil and dollars has to be stable and stability is maintained by various market interventions.

Stable oil-dollar-gold values mean that gold and oil will be undervalued.

Gold, if freed to price goods, would revalue everything upwards.

In a very real way, the dollar went onto an "oil standard" to replace the old "gold standard."

Another, March 24, 1998

Even today, so many years after these words were written, few understand that the dollar is valued and widely used because it buys oil. Shekels do not buy oil. Yuan do not buy oil. These can only buy dollars which then buys oil.

The deal between President Nixon and King Faisal to make dollars the Saudi oil settlement currency moved other oil markets to the same standard.

This makes dollars necessary and desirable. It creates a demand for dollars that other currencies do not enjoy.

If the dollar can be said to have any store of value it is in its oil purchasing power.

If your local currency be said to have any store of value it is in its dollar purchasing power which is also its oil purchasing power.

I view this US$ and say "how can it be of such value to all and have numbers as the stars in heaven"?

Another, April 4, 1998

Gold is limited, oil is limited, but the dollars in which their trades are settled are unlimited. And yet there is a kind of price stability in the triad.

This is our signal that a manipulation is at work.

Dollars are needed for international trade settlement generally and yet the number of settlements is finite while the number of dollars is infinite.

People value dollars as if their supply was limited and in fact the supply is unlimited. The supply grows larger every day, along with dollar paper issued by the Treasury.

This tension between reality and fantasy can only be resolved against the dollar.

Today, the world's currency, the US$, by default, would require a gold price of many, many thousands to back it without using its citizens as collateral!

Another, April 25, 1998

If we took away the dollar's reserve currency status, which is gained by being the medium for settling oil and gold trading, the only backing the dollar would have is the "full faith and credit" of the U.S. Government.

"Full faith and credit" means the intention to tax the future production of its citizens. That is the "collateral" of which *Another* speaks.

Taking the amount of dollars now in circulation, taking the amount of Treasury paper in circulation, adoption of a gold standard would require a sky-high price for gold in order to be apportioned sensibly.

One valuation of $10,000 an ounce has been developed by analyst James Turk and is gaining acceptance.

Now, to many of the "gold bugs" reading *Another* in 1998, this gold price of "many many thousands" signaled a *payday in fiat*. It signaled an adjustment that had to be made eventually once reality asserted itself on the government. It was how they were going to become rich - *in fiat*.

So many gold bugs are actually fiat bugs. They are recognized more and more as mere traders looking for a payoff in dollars.

But that is not the main point here. The main point is that the issuance of dollars is so out of kilter that it would take a gold value of thousands per ounce to match the U.S. gold supply against the U.S. dollar supply.

Another believed that nature's remedy, as seen in previous passages, would be the destruction of the dollar and all of its paper assets, and all of the world's paper currencies which are backed by dollars.

It seems more likely that gold backing would be applied to a new currency, not to the overextended dollar.

But, from an "oil producing" country, holding world class reserves, a low USD price offers all the advantages. It produces an ever dependent economic system, that, "in real terms of need" "upvalues all inground reserves" with a far higher "future need".

Another, March 21, 1998

Politically, there is much more to gain, by producing countries, by "managing" its [oil] price down, than by "allowing" its price to rise thru freemarket use!

Another, March 21, 1998

The MBAs have a term: "buying market share."

Buying market share will be profitable later. Meanwhile, a low price discourages domestic production, holding competitors in check, locking in customers.

Low price also creates political leverage which may be of greater value than lost revenues for an oil producer. Part of the Nixon-Faisal deal involved security guarantees for the Kingdom.

A low price can obtain more than money: defense pacts, arms sales, diplomatic favors, various kinds of market access, legitimacy and a seat at certain tables.

Today, many try to understand oil thru a currency that cannot offer a final payment of true value.

Another, April 26, 1998

This is a much simpler idea than it appears.

The end-of-day trading price in this or that benchmark is what we use to understand the value of oil. On that basis, refineries are built or mothballed, oil wells are opened or capped, "alternative energies" are priced, funded, subsidized, etc.

Oil is indispensable but consumed. Dollars are dispensable and never consumed, circulating endlessly, never sitting still, and never finite in their ever-growing supply.

The valuation of oil in dollars is the political outcome to a political deal.

Payment for oil is not "final" as the fiat has to be put to work as soon as collected and the true value of the oil is lost in the working of a politically-determined transaction executed in paper.

Gold would finalize the payment.

However, the oil market was never controlled to move the price higher! It was controlled to keep the price down! Even "back then", oil was managed in much the same way as gold is today.

Another, March 21, 1998

There is a persistent rumor, whenever oil prices rise, that the oil companies are manipulating prices upwards.

This ignores the overwhelming interests of everyone, everywhere in cheap oil. The world needs cheap oil and the powers that be realize they must keep it cheap or face unimaginable consequences.

At the time of the Nixon-Faisal deal for settling oil sales in dollars, U.S. production was meeting 70% of domestic needs. Thus, the U.S. was a net consumer of oil, like much of the world, and was politically invested in low prices.

Low prices could be achieved by political warnings to producers; by deals with producers; by stockpiling and releasing stockpiles; by issuing derivatives in excess of production; by short-selling without having underlying oil assets (naked shorting); by overstating reserves; by overstating new discoveries; and by investment in the development of new supplies.

The oil price suppression in various markets resembles the gold price suppression.

[G]old, while allowed to be "freely convertible" into any currency, is not allowed to trade "freely." Its price is managed. It is the "political metal!"

Another, March 7, 1998

There is an idea that central banks need gold to stay cheap in order to preserve the prestige of the local currency. This is probably not what interests *Another*.

In his view, the gold-oil-dollar triad breaks if any of these three elements becomes too expensive relative to the other. Breaking the linkage, as we have seen, would spell the end of the world's currency-based trading system.

In 1998, when this was written, central banks were going into their reserves and selling off their gold. Their holdings became heavily currency-weighted which created an additional incentive to keep the price of gold down in order to keep the value of their reserves up.

As this is written, central banks have been accumulating gold. The rise in gold prices has partially offset their losses in foreign currency values. In the case of the European Central Bank (ECB), the value of its reserves has actually increased overall because of the proportion of gold held. So the incentivization for gold holding in central banks is now reversed from what it was in 1998.

The continued suppression of gold prices, however, proves the point that central bank holdings do not drive gold price suppression.

Something else is at work and *Another* has tried to identify what that something is.

The Western governments needed to keep the price of gold down so it could flow where they needed it to flow.

Another, October 5, 1997

If, as rumors had it, oil prices were kept low in part by contracts that supplemented dollar payments with secret gold call options, then the gold needed to flow to oil producers.

Another was convinced that this was happening and that the Mid-East oil producers had accumulated significant gold through their oil trade. The blogger "FOFOA" has actually collected and published photo images of mainstream news stories from the period that refer to this link.

The point is simple: if it takes dollars plus gold to buy oil, keep the gold price down in order to keep the oil price down.

For the modern industrial economy, oil is not an option or a luxury. Gold, on the other hand, is something a modern economy can do without.

If *Another* is right and the gold flow is the reverse side of the oil flow, resale would further depress gold prices.

It does not appear that the oil states are selling off the gold they might earn from oil sales. In a dollar-plus-gold deal, that would work against their interests anyway.

You have C[entral] B[anks]s that highly value gold, but need its price in currencies to fall as a means of pricing oil.

Another, January 23, 1998

If gold prices rise in dollar terms, then selling less gold earns more dollars with which to buy more oil, right?

If higher gold prices cheapen dollars, does that mean cheaper oil?

Not so. The oil seller is not using dollars exclusively to discover the price of oil. He is not looking at the price of gold and the price of dollars and saying, "Gold is a liar, I'll use the dollars to value my oil."

The dollar value of gold is a check against the dollar value of oil.

Given a higher gold price, the oil producer wants gold or more dollars. Our incentive is to get more oil for fewer dollars.

The weaker gold appears, the stronger the dollar appears, and the more desirable as a medium of settlement for oil sales.

The central banks of the world are interested in a stronger dollar as well because the dollar is their reserve and oil sellers (until recently) will not accept non-dollar payments.

You have merchant banks creating a huge "digitized paper gold" market for trading only.

Another, January 23, 1998

Today, more gold is traded than exists!

Another, November 28, 1997

Paper gold, these investment bank creations, were just coming online as *Another* was posting his "Thoughts." Unlike futures, they did not have a settlement delivery dimension to them.

This creation produced a digitized claim to a share of warehoused gold. The gold was not redeemable, it simply backed the paper: unit of paper equals unit of gold.*

By making paper gold accessible through retail outlets, the investment banks cashed in on the public's desire to own gold. The public gained imaginary gold without having the "burden" of storing real gold. Paper exchanges gained an endless flow of transaction income from buying and selling gold in paper form.

This paper was then the basis of option derivatives, further expanding the paper gold supply.

The physical demand for gold was reduced by easy access to a substitute and this is reflected in gold pricing in public markets then and today.

In fact, since *Another* wrote this, the number of paper gold instruments has exploded, redirecting interest in physical gold away from open markets for physical metal.

* *This statement compresses the history of the redeemability of paper gold.*

There is no end to the amount of paper contracts that can be written and sold to drop the price of gold.

Another, November 3, 1997

Since the advent of "paper gold," the markets have allowed naked "short sales" of gold. The short seller, who is depressing the price, does not need to have underlying physical metal to take the short position. The only limit to the number of short positions to be taken against gold might be fear of losses.

But here too, market rules favor those shorting gold because the short position can be rolled over and losses deferred indefinitely.

Given enough cash to maintain the position, the seller of paper gold can keep going forever, even adding to the short position.

There is truly no end to the number of contracts that can short gold.

You have other CBs holding gold in the form of "paper commitments" and calling it physical.

Another, January 23, 1998

One form of these "paper commitments" is an IOU from bullion banks to central banks given in return for gold leased from the central banks. The current wisdom is that the bullion banks sold the gold they leased from the central banks, thus making these IOUs problematic.

As this is written, there are supply problems in the gold market as central banks call in their paper commitments by requiring the return of gold. The market lacks sufficient supplies of gold at current low prices to allow bullion banks to satisfy their obligations.

For example, much of the German state gold supply is held in New York by the New York Federal Reserve Bank. The German central bank has a paper commitment entitling it to what it stored there.

Absent restrictive clauses in the storage agreement, the New York Fed has been able to lease out Germany's gold, or use it as collateral for some other transaction, or even sell it (being on the hook to replace it by quantity and quality if ever called on to deliver).

Germany can publicly claim to hold a certain amount of (New York) gold and the New York Fed can claim to hold a certain amount of gold (that's really Germany's) and some central bank that leased Germany's gold from the Fed can claim to hold that gold itself.

This is a worst-case scenario though many on the gold scene today claim that this is the means by which gold is counted, double counted, and triple counted to produce a completely inflated idea of the amount of gold in circulation today.

Such an inflated idea of the gold supply further depresses gold's price in dollars because it overstates the supply.

You have some CBs having nothing to do with any of this and buying in the off market.

Another, January 23, 1998

In other words, you have central banks who are not playing paper games or staging fractional reserve operations with gold but who are accumulating physical gold in non-public markets.

Because the prices and quantities are traded "off market," they cannot help reveal a truer price for gold in the public markets.

An important part of *Another's* thinking is that there is a relatively small public market for gold pricing purposes and then there are private transactions on a scale that would dwarf public trading which are never made public, thus leaving the "public price" intact and subject to manipulations.

As this is written, it has been some years since the volume of all stock transactions on private electronic exchanges exceeded 70%. That means that the stock market indices we track are 30% complete, 30% representative of total pricing activity. As the volumes on public stock exchanges continue to collapse, more of the public will become aware of a tiered pricing issue in which the public values do not match the private values.

In 1998, *Another* proposed something similar was true for gold trading. Some CBs (he suggested Asian) were taking a completely different approach to gold than their counterparts.

Today, there is a gold flow from West to East. China's central bank is accumulating. Other Asian central banks appear to be doing the same, albeit on a smaller scale.

There is a limit to how far gold can be inflated in quantity using "fractional reserve leasing" as backing. The fatal flaw was found in the "forward sales" of unmined gold. The whole system counted on the expansion of cheap mining techniques to supply much more gold at a cheaper price far into the future.

Another, December 12, 1997

This is a comment made at a specific time that has timeless elements.

In the 1990s (into today), there was (and remains) a kind of paper gold that makes claims on mining companies' future gold output.

Up through the 1980s, there had been breakthroughs that made gold more accessible to miners and cheaper to mine. At the turn of the century, however, the advances slowed and the future became one of only small improvements in mining technology.

Another is saying that the volume of paper gold issued at one time matched high expectations of technology. This episode exposed a kind of pyramid effect in the paper gold market.

Now, a central bank can lease out or sell its gold. It could offset the lease or sale by buying an option to replace that amount of gold out of the future production of a mining firm. If the option cost less than the sale or lease of gold, the CB could pocket the difference and still claim gold reserves of the quantity that it leased out or sold.

The central banks fell victim to a tech bubble that generated inflated expectations of gold supplies. They leased out and sold their gold creating double and triple accounting for the quantity of gold held by the CBs.

They made a bet that more gold would be available for less money, that the gold they held now was "overpriced" against future supply.

They were wrong and today they are accumulating gold but the paper trail they left continues to inflate the amount of gold held and they continue to play leasing games that result in an overcounting of gold assets and an inflation effect similar to fractional reserve banking.

More gold has been sold than can ever be covered! This market is not the same as the past.

Another, November 22, 1997

The upshot of the central banks' leasing games is that more rights to gold have been sold (more IOUs issued) than can be covered by physical gold. At the time *Another* wrote this, the production options central banks once purchased also failed to offset the deficits.

The physical gold is completely overcommitted.

This makes possible a run on gold just as there might be a run on some failing currency. Currently, every crimp in market supplies is generating rumors of a run on physical gold.

Overcommitment also means the ratio of gold to paper has broken free of its anchor and is free-floating. Its value is notional and a detriment to pricing physical gold. It is a different animal altogether.

However, the two remain linked through the pricing of real gold in the USA through paper pricing on the COMEX exchange.

Your neighborhood gold dealer compensates for the mismatch by adding a premium to the price of physical gold to offset the distortion caused by paper gold pricing.

Another predicted that paper gold will burn with a dramatic rise in the rise of physical gold. A dramatic rise would break the pretense that paper represents real gold and it would cause a dramatic repricing of the paper downwards.

A dramatic rise in the real price of gold would follow a shortage of physical gold in one or more major markets.

Today, the public went "whole hog" for paper gold and has paid a great price. Wall Street invented this game from the previous war as a way of keeping customer "gold money" in house!

Another, November 28, 1997

Gold and real currency have been replaced by paper substitutes.

In the current investment climate, the security of gold has magically become the security of paper somehow connected to gold.

Previously, investors buying gold were not buying paper. They were outside of the financial markets.

With the advent of paper gold, Wall Street can reap transaction costs (and other income) from interest in gold.

Speculators can get in and out of "gold" positions quickly; they also have a range of derivatives available to trade based on some underlying paper gold vehicle.

Wall Street is not the only venue for paper gold. Advertisements now air for paper gold that can be added to workers' retirement accounts.

Retirement accounts: there is no public hog more whole than that.

Looking back, one will ask, "how could I have thought that no one wanted gold, when more of it was being bought than existed?"

Another, December 07, 1997

This is the future lament of an investor who is all in paper.

Such an investor has reached certain conclusions about gold. That investor rejects gold based on what he was told and believes.

An "enlightened" American will have been informed by the very best experts that a 5-7% allocation of gold is the appropriate "hedge" against all the paper he owns.

Now, the very best experts do not distinguish between paper gold and physical gold, so the "enlightened" American may be invested 95% in paper paper and 5% in gold paper!

Such an "enlightened" one will wonder why he did not allocate more funds into physical gold, should the worst comes to pass.

We judge demand by looking at the buying and selling. Much more gold is being bought than exists or can be produced.

This is a fact that has not been absorbed since *Another* made it clear in 1997. It is known on the fringes of the investment community but is not known by investors at large.

Waste no more time on paper gold, you have suffered enough. Play paper games no more, as the future of your family waits a decision.

Another, December 07, 1997

If you believe certain things about gold, do not transfer those beliefs to paper gold. If gold has value, assess that value differently than you do paper gold.

When paper burns, your family will suffer, should you be in paper.

Paper is a trading medium. Paper provides the chits we use in the great casino that markets have become.

Gold, the store of value, is intergenerational wealth.

5. Hidden Transactions

Understand that oil is still traded for a certain number of US$ but after the deal is done a certain amount of gold is also purchased "with the future flow of oil as collateral." If the world price of gold gets too high, then the oil price is falling. So long as gold stays cheap in currency terms oil will be in good supply.

Another, October 7, 1997

Another writes in a compressed style. This transaction of gold for oil could be structured exactly as described above or it could be shorthand for an option contract of some sort.

In an options contract that matches this description, you would want the optionality of a gold sale (at a special price) linked to the optionality of future oil flow. The terms and conditions we may never know.

The way *Another* describes this exchange, it seems the gold would have to be sold into a continuous oil flow rather than in one settlement.

At the time this was written, central banks had gold stockpile legacies at a time when academic opinion found no use for gold. There was gold to sell and no stigma attached to selling gold.

Since sovereign oil is bought and sold privately by and large (to refineries, etc.), the gold sales seem likely to be parallel government-to-government transactions.

These exchanges may have been a limited to Another's time of writing or they may continue in some form today.

One can gain more wealth by keeping oil down than by driving it up, much more! And what is the value of this type of manipulation? It is measured in gold!

Another, November 22, 1997

This statement looks difficult but simply ties in to the gold-oil parallel sale discussed previously.

With the oil price kept low, gold is sold at a discount to guarantee oil supplies at lower prices. The sovereign oil seller can accumulate gold, which is in limited supply, for oil, of which the seller has an immense supply.

If oil were to find its price in a free market, there would be no sense in supplementing that exchange with a gold sale.

In this sense, giving the world the cheap oil it needs gains the permanent wealth of gold to the oil seller.

Another gave a specific example of this on November 21, 1997:

> In the early 1990s oil went to $30++ for reasons we all know. What isn't known is that its price didn't drop that much. You see the trading medium changed. Oil went from $30++ to $19 + X amount of gold! Today it costs $19 + XXX amount of gold! Yes, gold has gone up and oil has stayed the same in most eyes.

In this example, more wealth was gained by keeping oil down, as the gold rider on the oil price increased from x to xxx.

Without real physical to supply the oil states, they WILL bid for gold with oil! The BIS [Bank for International Settlements] will do the only thing they can, halt all trading and declare gold a "world oil currency"! To that end, all forms of paper gold will burn. How long till this starts?

Another, November 28, 1997

Here, *Another* takes us into the heart of the oil-gold-dollar nexus. "Without real physical" gold available for purchase with dollars, oil states will use their own oil to bid directly for gold, without dollars as a medium of exchange.

Now, the BIS is the central banks' central bank where dollar reserves play the major role in transacting central bank business. If the dollar cannot buy gold and the oil producers will not sell for dollars but rather bid oil against gold, settlement among central banks would have to be made in gold. This decision would flow downhill to commercial banks and markets.

The danger to the world currency system here is that oil would be marked to the gold market and gold would be marked to the oil market, with no dollars involved.

The Bank of International Settlement (BIS) also currently handles the central banks' gold transactions. It is already set up to enable gold's use to settle oil trades.

Current BIS gold operations are gold for dollars, dollars for gold and gold for gold. But in a world where oil equals gold, the current transactions are meaningless and would need to be frozen in order to enable gold owners to settle oil purchases.

Using gold to oil trading would destroy the paper gold market. The valuation of gold would be marked to oil. Paper gold will burn because it has a dollar link but no direct oil link and because its allocated gold (if it holds any) now serves an entirely different purpose.

You will not see 80% or more of gold deals. If it was done with all to see the discount value would be lost as the world price would explode.

Another, Dec ember 12, 1997

Another mentioned gold sales as supplementing oil sales and of course these deals would be kept private and their pricing would fall outside of what is recorded in the public precious metal markets.

In other writings, *Another* has said that the small quantities of physical gold traded in public markets reflect a public price for small quantities of gold. He notes that the really large quantities that change hands are subject to negotiation and that an entirely different pricing system comes into play for large, off-the-books trades.

The public price, which applies to the restricted public volumes of the metals exchanges represents a "discount value." The discount is achieved through price suppression.

The private price carries a premium in respect to the public price, a kind of "reality premium."

Another mentions that if we knew what gold was trading for privately, "the world price would explode." This is not an outcome to be wished for, necessarily, because the markets would break down with bidders finding no askers.

The 80% figure is interesting in light of today's stock market trading. As of 2010, 70% of stock trading was done privately at prices never recorded in the exchanges.

In the real world some people know that gold is real wealth no matter what currency price is put on it. Around the world it is traded in huge volumes that never show up on bank statements, gov[ernment] stats, or trading graph paper.

Another, October 5, 1997

In separate writings, *Another* has suggested he might have been involved in such transactions and that they involved both states and private individuals ("giants"). His area of operations seemed to be Asia, although no hints he gave were clear.

But let us try to understand "huge volumes" just from public or semi-public records.

One venue for the trading of physical gold is the London Bullion Market Association (LBMA) "over-the-counter" (OTC) gold market. The Gold Anti-Trust Action Committee looked at the LBMA daily trading volumes for November 2009 (available on the LBMA's website). Some 2,100 metric tonnes of gold were changing owners *every day*. At the then price of $1,150/oz, this would have been a $77 billion value. This dwarfed the oil market at a ratio of 3/2.

In an article written in 2010, The Gold Anti-Trust Action Committee writes,

> There is a myth among even knowledgeable gold investors and analysts that the gold market is tiny, but in reality it is the biggest physically traded commodity market in the world. The perception of gold being a tiny market comes from the tiny annual production of gold. Global gold production is only 2,200 metric tonnes per year, which is equivalent to the gross trade in gold on the LBMA in just one day.

The LBMA volume figures were not available when *Another* wrote this thought about volumes. The LBMA numbers may fulfill his statement of fact or he may have had in mind even larger volumes of (off the books) gold trading.

... the price of gold is dropping precisely because "too many people are buying it"! Think now, if you are a person of "great worth" is it not better for you to acquire gold over years, at better prices?

Another, January 10, 1998

Imagine that you are a person of great worth trying to accumulate gold. Your best bargain would be to buy at the suppressed price over time in the limited volume public markets. You would need years to hit your accumulation targets but your averaged price in currency would be very cheap.

By the same token, you and others would have every incentive to suppress the price further.

In the public sphere, those paying for oil with gold would need access to cheap gold. Likewise, central banks accumulating modest quantities of gold would want a suppressed price for their transactions.

These are the “many”: oil producers, short sellers, paper gold traders and dealers, private accumulators, industry, central banks.

The need for publicly available cheaper gold can work to the good of some.

The world has changed and left most goldbugs fighting the last war!

Another, November 2, 1997

Another posted this comment on a gold forum and was reacting generally to the comments he saw.

- The gold bugs of that time (and perhaps this one) focused on hyperinflationary threats rather than sudden currency destruction.
- They tended to look at the domestic money supply and not the oil dollars that would rush home if the dollar standard was abandoned.
- They invested in mining stocks and other forms of paper gold not understanding that they were lowering the price of what they wanted to see rise.
- They focused on a return to the gold standard not realizing that the dollar was on an oil standard.
- They projected a common fate for silver and other precious metals, even creating "historical ratios" expressed in dollars.
- They saw gold as a pathway to sound money (stable exchange) rather than as a (store of) value in itself.

Too many gold bugs are currency traders. They hope to get "rich" (in fiat!) by selling their gold for currency at a good price. They should be called "fiat bugs" really.

Thanks to the work of *Another*, the better class of gold bug is now fighting future wars. The discussion board commenter Friend of *Another* (FOA) tried to apply *Another's* thinking to different problems. The blogger FOFOA (Friend of a Friend of Another) likewise uses *Another's* Thoughts as a touchstone for exploring new ideas. The Gold Anti-Trust Action Committee and others fight to expose price suppression.

Many gold bugs, however, are still fighting the last war even today.

6. Paper Profits and Paper Gold

Participants have yet to realize that the gold futures, gold options and gold forward markets, worldwide, have become little more than currency trading arenas. The percentage of gold delivered against these markets has grown so small as to be nonexistence when compared to actual metal settled at closing.

Another, March 7, 1998

Another is NOT saying that they are currency exchanges, in the sense of FX markets, but rather that they are arenas in which fiat money changes hands with profit and losses being taken in paper currency.

In these "paper gold" markets, traders win or lose paper, not gold.

In 1998, so few traders were taking delivery of physical metal, *Another* was tempted to use the word "nonexistence" to describe the physical market represented by these trades.

Today, some metals markets reserve the right to settle delivery requirements in metal or in currency but at their discretion.

Taking the metal out of the trade and setting it on the sidelines this way marginalizes the exchange as a metal market and as a way to discover gold prices.

This seems to be one very effective way to disconnect the price of "paper gold" from physical gold.

Another's oft-repeated point was that stress placed on the gold trading system or the currency regime would break the paper gold markets' tenuous link to physical gold prices.

More gold has been sold than can ever be covered! This market is not the same as the past.

Another, November 22, 1997

This radical statement from 1997 is now the common wisdom today. It refers to all types of uncovered transactions.

- There are the miner production futures that build in assumptions about technology enhancements that will increase outputs.
- There are the sales of paper gold instruments that are not backed by or redeemable by gold holdings.
- There are the central banks leasing out gold in the manner of fractional reserve banking.
- There is the nominally illegal sale and/or leasing of bonded or allocated gold.
- There is all the double-counting and overestimating associated with these games.

As this is written, certain states, such as Germany and Venezuela, are recalling their bullion from repositories abroad.

There is concern that the gold is not where it is supposed to be.

More important, however, is *Another's* point that the market is no longer *one for one* as it once may have ben. One unit of gold now supports many (very many!) derivatives, contracts, leases, borrowings, and collateralized transactions.

As fiat is "pyramided" by fractional reserve banking, so one single ounce of gold may have thousands of paper claims laid against it. These claims cannot be satisfied.

Sir, a day will come, when those who have sold gold they do not own, will be forced to buy it back. It is the nature of men, to once in life do a foolish deed for gain. Some walk away, with understanding. Some stay too long and are made to walk low without wealth. Today, our world is fat with stolen profits in a paper world, even as poor ones starve.

Another, March 8, 1998

One of the enduring ideas of the gold and silver bugs, then and now, is that the overhang of paper commitments, especially short selling, will allow a massive "squeeze" where the shorts "will be forced to buy back" gold. Many today think that the next major rise in gold prices will occur when this squeeze finally occurs.

Here *Another* notes the squeeze as likely (or inevitable). This was not the way he envisioned a major rise in gold, however. The thought presented here is a moral reflection.

If we consider the amount of uncovered gold transactions that have been entered into, the amount of fractional gold lending that goes on, as well as the allocation games that are played, we may believe that a squeeze on the short interest will be coming.

In recent times, in the silver markets, there was a popular movement to break the exchanges by taking delivery of the metal. This attempted short squeeze failed.

In the gold markets, however, where the scale of operations is so much larger, the forces that compel buy-back will not be engineered by traders settling in gold but by world historical forces.

Meanwhile, the gold analyst Jim Willie has been saying for some time that entities in Asia are draining western gold supplies by taking delivery and by putting pressure on the weaker bullion banks. He calls them "the new sheriffs in town" who want to ensure that those gaming the market will eventually "walk low without wealth." If Jim Willie is correct, this behavior is more a threat to the banking system than to the paper gold trading system.

The profits stolen by short selling will continue until "paper burns" and it will not end with a modest "short squeeze."

After [a] long search, what you may find will be a "paper deed" to gold that is many times over "encumbered" from much use and travels through foreign hands!

Another, June 14, 1998

Here, *Another* is picturing an outcome where the gold owner does not possess the physical metal. The "long search" may refer to legal battles or arbitrated claims.

Already, in 1998, some gold owners were placing their metal in the hands of counterparties. These counterparties charged storage fees and issued receipts for the gold. "Unallocated" gold guaranteed a like amount could be returned to the owner. "Allocated" gold was not to be disturbed and its serial numbers were listed so the same units could be returned as were stored.

The rumor mill of today has caught up with *Another*.

It is said that gold depositors have lodged lawsuits against Swiss banks to recover clear title to their own gold that they thought was being stored but which was actually being loaned, leased, or sold. One colorful anecdote has allocated gold being claimed by the owner and showing unexpected serial numbering.

This is a micro level statement of the problem, however.

Another suggested that this was happening on the interbank level, on the central bank level, and on the exchange holdings level.

He is saying that multiple claims on the existing gold stocks creates an unstable situation.

Think of mortgages that are endlessly resold and packaged into derivatives.

Or think of a property with many liens on it. That would be gold represented by a paper claim.

No form of paper wealth will survive the financial crush once the CBs stop selling! NOTHING!

Another, October 9, 1997

In writing this, *Another* had commented that the London Bullion Market Association (LBMA) had managed to corner the physical gold market. In this scenario, physical gold would have to make its way into the market through Central Bank (CB) sales - and in 1997, CBs were certainly selling.

This selling, in *Another's* view, kept the oil-dollar-gold nexus alive. A true corner, should the CBs run out of gold, would explode the gold price and thus destroy the dollar and its dependent world currencies.

One might ask, "As long as one could sell gold one doesn't have as well as various forms of paper gold, how could a corner matter?'

A corner in gold would matter if any part of the oil trade were settled in gold delivery. If the oil to gold price (expressed in dollars) went out of equilibrium, oil producers would be incentivized to price oil in gold, not dollars.

The result would be a "financial crush."

The corner did not happen. Central banks are now net buyers, not sellers, but gold is still flowing.

Further, the paper gold market has exploded in size and volume since *Another* wrote these words, and it is soaking up much demand that would limit the supply of physical through the buying of bullion.

The crush has not come but the supply threat remains.

It [paper] is a strange way to hold wealth. One might say "my net worth is the intention of others to pay me a credit from someone else".

Another, November 2, 1997

All of my paper has at least one counterparty. Usually it has multiple counterparties. There is a chain of intentions that has to be fulfilled for me to receive my payment.

If I receive my payment, it will be in currency, which has a government counterparty.

The dollar is a credit, a promise to pay by the U.S. Government. The "full faith and credit" of the government backing the dollar is based on the power to tax.

This is the case with most fiat money.

It is in this sense that even paper money represents an eventual intention to make good on value through the taxpayer ("someone else").

The "permanence" of the value of the paper money depends in part on (1) the continued intention of the government ("others") to pay you the credit you claim and (2) the taxpayer ("someone else") supplying what is needed to fulfill the government's intention.

The dollar, the "greenback," began as U.S. Treasury paper - a promise to pay. Like any other bond, note, or bill, the dollar has built into it "counterparty risk." Whomever holds a dollar has two counterparties that must make good for the dollar to have value. These counterparties are the government and the taxpayer.

Gold, of course, has no counterparty risk. Its value does not depend on the intentions of others to honor commitments.

Think now in light of the real world around us. Hold your assets in the sun of day, what do we see? A government bond denominated in a currency? Now, remove the currency from the bond, show what is in your hand? Hear me now, we see nothing of "productive use"!

Another, February 7, 1998

The promise of a government bond is to pay the bearer currency.

The government that issues the bond issues the currency.

If the government were unable to pay the currency or if the currency became worthless, of what value would the bond be? What kind of claim would it represent?

Some states have tried to answer this question by issuing their bonds paying the currency of some other state. This is useful where the people have little faith in the government's own bonds but it increases risk because now the state must find the foreign currency to pay its bonds.

And of course, the foreign currency may become worthless or hard to obtain.

Visit a coin shop and you will see for sale paper bonds that have no more "productive use" except as decorations or souvenirs.

For the future of most, "the wealth that was shown in paper" will be seen as clouds in the sky!

Another, February 22, 1998

Separate the thought (the value of a currency) from the paper (issued by the central bank or treasury) and what is left? Something perhaps even more ephemeral than clouds.

Another here says wealth "shown in paper." We can add that in many cases it is shown in electronic records that refer to paper, which in turn refers to units of currency, which in turn refer to values expressed in the buying and selling of markets driven by government currency wars and "the dirty float."

The cloud has no staying power, neither does paper wealth.

"For the future of most" can refer to us but it certainly refers to future generations.

In this day, as not in the past, the loss of paper value as a concept will destroy the very foundation of wealth that this economic system is built on. This drama has started and is well underway!

Another, February 14, 1998

The world of 1998 had reached a pinnacle of material wealth historically, while that wealth rested on paper embodying a concept. Moreover, the use of "conceptual paper" as wealth was universal.

So, lose the concept, lose the wealth, lose the economy worldwide.

Another says this had started.

One thing he had noticed at the popular level was that non-Westerners were re-evaluating gold as money and were accumulating gold locally regardless of prices set in Western markets. He said people were turning away from the current Western thinking about gold.

Another also wrote of transactions to accumulate large stocks of gold outside of the established (Western) venues. He was indirect in this but appears to have been referring to (non-Western) men of wealth as well as (non-Western) governments.

Another noticed different trade and monetary experiments designed to sidestep the dollar settlement system. He noted the creation of the Euro as an alternative reserve currency. His students have noted the presence of gold in the mix of reserves held by the European Central Bank and they have made much of the ECB's decision to price that gold to market rates rather than to an artificially low fixed rate, like other central banks.

The revaluation of gold in relation to paper currencies would inevitably damage the paper value concept.

Some say, "I hold investments of great increase these past years, and am much ahead of the inflation, if it should come." I say, "Your investments, worldwide, have moved little, as it has been the currencies that denominate your assets that fall a great deal."

Another, May 26 1998

My company sold the same number of widgets in Canada this year as last year but this year the Canadian dollar is worth more. I show profits!

To put it a different way, my company sold the same number of widgets in Canada but this year the USD is worth less. I show profits!

This idea is well understood today as American corporations post quarterly profits that represent *no more than their foreign earnings in foreign currencies as expressed in the exchange rate of the ever-weakening dollars.*

If the dollar declines, the company needs to sell no more abroad than the previous quarter to show an increase in revenue.

"Paper profits" are earned by selling in overseas markets while the dollar is weakening.

International companies have become exchange rate players and have a stake in their governments' currency wars.

7. Trading Gold

Physical gold should be purchased for a lifetime holding, not a trade.

Another, March 7, 1998

It is not for "the investment", it is as the "conclusion of wealth."

Another, August 11, 1998

So much of the commentary on the gold market is made by traders.

For instance, as this is written there are predictions that gold will reach $2,500/oz by the end of the year. Some are predicting $5,000/oz within two years. It is not uncommon to hear the current "real" value given as $10,000 or $12,000/oz.

If you are "keeping score" in fiat currency, some part of your mind is looking for a fiat payday.

When gold's value in fiat skyrockets, are you going to trade your gold for wheelbarrows of currency? They say that in Weimar, gold could be had for dollars but not for marks. There were bids in marks but no asks.

Now, if you owned a great estate, filled with fine paintings, surrounded by exquisite gardens, appointed with collectible furniture, would you be running to the assessors every day for the latest uptick in value? Would you have endless appraisals of the paintings and sculptures, the silver and crystal?

Or, when someone asks you what your magnificent estate is worth, would you answer "I have no idea?"

You would have no idea and be perfectly satisfied not to know.

Such a mind can only see value in paper terms. For such thought finds gold as wealth, only if it is someday turned back to paper! Paper, indeed!

Another, February 7, 1998

This is the most difficult thing for the gold bug to understand because we are all trained to value things in fiat. When we say "gold has gone up," what follows is a dollar figure. To "profit" from the rise against fiat, the gold holder would have to sell gold in exchange for fiat.

The goldbug constantly reads tips from people telling how to "score big" (in fiat). Some goldbugs fantasize about what they will buy when they cash out of their gold position.

Moreover, what goldbug, living in the West, thinks intergenerationally? Here in the West, there is no family, or a broken family, or there may be multiple families from multiple marriages enjoying a very loose, clan-like structure.

There may be no heirs or there may be too many heirs. There is no intergenerational impetus. Get yours now. Grab it while you can.

The goldbug has also learned that hoarding is evil. Savers have been wearing black hats since the early 20th Century and the theories of John Maynard Keynes dominated economics. Currently, there is a war on savers in which they are paid less than one percent while inflation is targeted by the government to rise to two percent.

The goldbug is part of a larger consumer culture: eat, drink, be merry.

So, the goldbug wants a payday.

That makes this idea very hard: gold is the conclusion of wealth. Only gold is wealth. Cash and stocks are transitional media that may come to rest in real wealth, gold, if the right choices are made.

The cash I do not need to work for me anymore goes into wealth, stored value, and there it lies still.

... as it is not "what we sell gold for, but rather how much gold can one buy" that produces wealth over time!

Another, June 6 1998

The cash I do not need to work for me anymore goes into wealth, stored value, and there it lies still.

Another has inverted the goldbug's sense of value: if I am plotting how much fiat I can earn on a gold trade, then my gold is valued in fiat.

But if I am plotting how much gold I can buy with my fiat, my fiat is valued in gold.

Here's another inversion, and it must have been shocking to the goldbugs of 1998:

- *A gold investment is not producing wealth over time!*
- *The continuous conversion of fiat into gold is producing wealth over time!*

Think about this: it is the act of accumulation that is creating wealth, not a buy-and-hold market timing strategy.

The buy-and-hold crowd may get a boost from an exchange rate tick or a commodities bubble or a miner's strike. This is not wealth and the "profits" will have to go back to work somehow, even if spent on pleasure.

Gold is wealth. Accumulation is wealth over time.

Know this, my knowledge of gold is for the simple ones of small thought, such as I. Resist the trader's mind, hold your wealth close. There are those that will take your worth at the very time you need it most. Most will not see the time or place, few are allowed!

Another, January 23 1998

The tale of a trader: you bought low and sold high. You sold your gold for bags full of fiat. Lucky you. But now all paper markets are burning.

What to do? Here is an economic crisis. You never needed gold more than now but you've sold it.

We of small minds have weak hands. Those with strong hands will want our gold and will make market events happen that shake our gold loose and into their pockets.

There will be bear raids and bull drives that promise payoffs but in fiat.

Resist the trader's mind. We will not foresee the time or place when our gold will be needed most.

During the time that must come, all forms of paper ownership of things will come into question.

Another, March 7 1998

Some collect gold for the wealth of future generations.

Some collect out of belief in *the time that must come*.

The trap, the paradox is that as such time draws near, as the ownership of paper becomes more and more dubious, those who value gold in fiat will see fiat prices rise to a point that tempt selling.

And at that time when all forms of paper ownership come into question, the gold trader will be holding only paper. Won't that be an astonishing sight?

How will paper come into question?

- The institutions behind paper may fail
- Counterparties may repudiate obligations or go bankrupt
- Asset holders may steal the assets or transfer them lawlessly
- New rules may be issued
- New paper may replace the old
- Values may be reset by force
- Some paper may be outlawed
- Some paper may be altered in terms and conditions
- There could be a boycott or embargo or blockade.

We say *the time that must come* out of a sense of history, not just because of this or that event. If everything were fairytale perfect with no cloud on the horizon, there would still be a time that must come.

Unlike the past, this market has an end. And this end will not be for those who have waited to buy!

Another, December 7 1997

Will you bid $1,000 when your broker screen shows $475? I myself, as a country will be "there!" You sir, will stand well behind most in line.

Another, April 18 1998

This public market in gold is subject to manipulation that will eventually end. The end will be marked, as *Another* has written elsewhere, by bids with no asks.

This he illustrates here with the broker screen scenario. Here the bid shows $475/oz but there are no sellers. *Another* will move ahead of the queue with bid numbers that test the point where the sellers may want to sell. We will be waiting for our $475 order to be filled when gold is trading much higher.

In our current reality, the broker's screen shows an official price from the official trading centers while large amounts of gold are changing hands at much higher prices in private deals.

The high bids are coming from the East both now and when *Another* wrote this.

[*Another says "as a country" he'll be there at the higher price. It is believed that he was at this time a gold market operator acting on behalf of some state's interests. This was the basis of his insights into large, off-the-books transactions at above market prices.*]

As long as there is an open market for gold, it will not be allowed to trade above its commodity price! It has far too much value for that to happen. You see, in much the same way that a zero coupon bond trades at a discount to face, gold is traded for its discount of money value to commodity price!

Another, November 16 1997

A bond has coupons which are clipped off and mailed in to receive an interest payment. At the end of the life of the bond, the complete principal is paid to the bondholder.

A zero coupon bond has no coupons and pays no interest. It has a face value (principal amount) that pays off on its maturity date. A thirty-year zero issued today will pay $1,000 in 2043. But it will not trade for $1,000 tomorrow, it will trade for much less. The market will determine how much less.

The bond with a future payoff of $1,000 may trade at $100 today.

So here *Another* describes a parallel situation between gold prices and zero coupon bond prices. The zero coupon bond has a maturity date. The maturity date provides a discounting factor.

Gold's maturity date is unknown, so the commodity price provides a discounting factor.

These money printers, they do much and fool no one. "Follow in the footsteps of giants", as they take in real gold. Do so and the future will show your wisdom from today!

Another, April 18 1998

Who are the giants? They are the wealthy with non-Western attitudes towards gold. They are those governments accumulating gold.

Both parties are buying gold at currently suppressed prices.

We can be like them, accumulating gold at the same public, suppressed prices, at the full commodity discount, and in that way "follow in the footsteps of giants."

When the future reveals *that time that must come*, the gold collector's wisdom will also be revealed.

8. The Value of Gold

Gold! It is the only medium that currencies do not "move thru". It is the only Money that cannot be valued by currencies. It is gold that denominates currency.

Another, January 23 1998

Currencies move through stocks, bonds, derivatives, commodities; fiat never sits still. Currency spent on gold has moved on but it has left value behind. The value of currency then is "How much gold can it buy?"

This is beginning to be understood and we see it in some new strains of gold commentary.

One analyst has noted that there remains an implicit ratio between the Gross Domestic Product (a proxy for size of the economy) and a nation's gold holdings. In other words, central banks maintain an indirect gold peg to their currencies. This is said to motivate their buying and selling of gold, at least to some extent.

An interesting theory about the current gold market is that among the major economies of the world, China's shows the grossest imbalance between gold reserves and GDP. The gold price is being suppressed to allow China time to accumulate sufficient gold to allow it to achieve the same GDP-bullion ratios of other countries. Once China's imbalance is fixed, or nearly fixed, the nations can revalue their currencies in a new international monetary agreement such as Bretton Woods without serious disadvantage to China.

The Dutch central banker Jelle Zijlstra, in his memoirs, refers to central bank revaluation as "putting a bit more gold in your currency."

This idea, whatever its merits, suggests that even states may believe in the gold basis of currency.

No one can see the value of a real asset when knowing how many currency units it is denominated in. Value is only known when holding one real asset next to another real asset and comparing the currency unit valuations of both.

Another, February 7 1998

With no replacement for the use of oil (at present to lower prices) and no "needed" use for gold in today's thought, we have the ingredients for a mismatch in value of epic proportions!

Another, January 17 1998

...if one can only see value in paper currency terms then one cannot see value at all.

Another, November 21, 1997

This brings us back to the oil-dollar-gold nexus.

The dollar producer needs oil.

The oil producer wants gold but will accept dollars or a dollar-gold combination for oil.

The dollar acts as an oil accounting unit. If the dollar begins to fail as such, some sort of new gold-backed settlement will likely emerge.

The mismatch *Another* referred to can be stated this way: in the world of 1998, gold was unwanted (look at the prices!) and oil was irreplaceable.

This mismatch created opportunities for oil providers to buy gold on the cheap. As *Another* said, it enabled gold to flow where it was needed.

How does one recognize real money? My answer is, find the largest store of financial units, held by banks, that is not lent out and does not earn interest. It is by far, gold!

Another, March 7 1998

This store of financial units is measured in weight and is, of course, gold.

Since this was written, we have become aware that banks have, in fact, been leasing out gold (including gold they do not have) and in that sense, gold has been "earning interest" in fiat.

In *Another's* time, leasing was assumed but not proven. Today it has been proven in the statements of central bankers but we still do not know the extent of leasing operations.

Another's point is that on their scale of monetary operations, and based on the type of monetary operations, we can see banks (and central banks) seem to value gold more than they value their own currency.

For many, the years have passed and this noble metal has not revealed the value it hides.

Another, June 29, 1998

What is the "return on this investment"? It cannot be known until time to collect, yes? Perhaps, a fortunate person will find "never a return."

Another, September 3, 1998

Gold will only have to be repriced once, that will be more than enough"!

Another, November 3 1997

The physical gold, this money insurance, it will be collected in future. In that time, the return will be easy to see.

Another, September 9, 1998

Another is NOT speaking to the "trader mind" here. The trader's mind prices gold in currency. The price of gold is "known" in dollars and the trader has seen gold go from $35/oz in the 1970s to something in the $350 range in the late 1990s. That return on investment can be calculated.

In this sense, the trader has seen the value gold hides, its value in currency, and is in a state of anxiety about how much more currency value is hidden.

If he sells too early he won't maximize his return on investment. He won't earn enough fiat!

As long as gold is priced in currency, its value will remain hidden. *Another* has said it needs to be priced against something of value.

Gold also has a transcendent value. This is the value that will be revealed "when paper burns." This storehouse of value will then be "priced," though not in currency.

The circumstances that would require we collect on our gold investment would be dire. This is why the wise person would be happy never to score a return on gold's hidden value.

I ask you, how can currency price gold? Indeed, no price will work!

Another, November 23 1997

In this modern world, the current value of every asset is formed by a relationship of gold/currencies/oil. This cross relationship is the "very basis of our modern world banking system"!

Another, April 18 1998

You see, in real world, gold is money, oil is money. But paper currency, it is only a receipt for commerce.

Another, April 19 1998

Currency, a medium of exchange, cannot price gold, a store of value, except to express a relationship between gold and something else of value.

Our modern banking system deals in these "paper receipts" for trades encompassing oil and gold and everyday spending.

Because oil producers are willing to take "paper receipts" (possibly with gold options), the world has a reserve currency: dollars.

Because there is a world reserve currency, other fiat currencies are practical.

The car you buy: its price is expressed in fiat which hearkens back to the dollar and the dollar is an expression of the gold-oil price ratio.

The dollars (or other fiat) circulating in your economy become "receipts" to be used again and again.

Should the links among gold, oil and dollars be disturbed, the modern world banking system would be in peril.

A day will come, sir, when no paper dollar will pry gold from your hands! In that day, you will be too smart for such foolishness.

Another, November 23 1997

Here, *Another* is writing for gold buyers with "trader minds."

Those who think like traders are looking for a sell point that maximizes their fiat payout for investing in gold.

But consider: the greater the dollar return on gold, the more desperate will be the fate of fiat at that point. When you can get a trillion dollars for an ounce of gold, what will a trillion dollars buy?

What will the world look like on the day of the maximum dollar payout?

Whether you like it or not, at the selling point where you decide to exchange your gold for dollars, life will force you to reprice your dollar "profits" into a third item or commodity in order to mentally "value" your profit.

This is because you must consider what you can do with those dollar profits.

And if you consider that question before your sale of gold, it seems likely that *no amount of paper dollars will be worth such a trade.*

I offer this consideration to all, would oil or gold hold the same currency price if no paper future market existed? Think long and hard on this, if oil and gold were bought and sold "marked to the market" physical for cash, would the USD price stay the same in todays' economy?

Another, March 21, 1998

This is a key part of the new thinking among today's gold buyers, a realization that markets in "paper gold" drain off the appreciation of gold's value by diverting investors.

The same would be true for oil, silver and other items of value.

The point is underlined when these paper exchanges write and rewrite their own rules to allow settlement at delivery to be made in cash rather than kind. Many of them will not deliver gold at the end of a gold contract.

It is interesting to see how many different paper gold instruments have appeared in the market since 1998, when *Another* wrote this.

Indications are that (a) there is money to be made in people's interest in gold and/or (b) there is money that would be bidding up the price of gold if more and more of these instruments didn't keep popping up.

So to rephrase *Another's* observation, imagine if the gold interest had nowhere to buy except in physical metal? The fiat price of gold would be astonishing.

To ask, "how can one afford $30,000 gold" would sound as today as "how can anyone afford $30,000 in savings account"? One does earn money, not afford it, yes?

Another, March 26, 1998

I spend part of my earned wages on gold and then store my gold money.

That sentence is very hard to understand using the trader mind because the trader has spent earned money on an *investment* called gold. My gold is not an investment it is money, better money than the fiat I earned on the job.

There is a second angle to this.

Assume the price of gold has reached an "astonishing" level, say $30,000/oz. It would be a very confused gold buyer who could not buy fractions of an ounce or gram. So why the question: "How can I afford expensive gold?"

The question seems to demand cheap gold for cheap buyers. But gold will find its own level.

And as *Another* points out, the form of the question is as silly as asking, "But how can anyone afford a brokerage account (or a house or an automobile, etc.).

This metal is sold with the "modern concept" of "gold is the commodity for fabrication" and "is dead as money" in "this new era."

Another, August 19, 1998

Here, *Another* is referring specifically to the mindset of the West. The gist of it is in America's Federal Reserve chairman saying that gold is not money and that central banks hold it as a reserve because of "tradition."

That chairman was trying to convey the general opinion of his peer group. The common reference to gold as a "barbarous relic" by leading economists permeates the world of banking, academia, and even the markets. The analyst James Grant likes to say that we have exchanged a gold standard for a PhD standard.

It is easier for economists to estimate future demand for gold if it is tied to some specific use, to industry inputs and outputs. Economics became a kind of central planning and as such deals in those kinds of matters.

Conventional opinion today recognizes an interest in gold far beyond its use in jewelry and circuitry but it does not know how to quantify this interest into predictive models. This aspect of gold is beyond our central planners.

Since *Another* wrote this, the world has moved on from viewing gold strictly as a commodity, an input. It still views gold being "dead as money."

Gold has not changed, nor has it lost its place in the world as money. It is still the test of currencies, yesterday, today and tomorrow!

Another, September 3, 1998

Gold remains money. This is why central banks hold gold as a reserve, not because of "tradition" as asserted by the U.S. Federal Reserve Chairman.

During the crisis of the Euro (ongoing at this writing), the European Central Bank (ECB) saw the value of its reserves increase. This is because of the large proportion of those reserves (20%) held in gold. As the value of the foreign currency reserves declined, the value of its gold holdings rose more than enough to offset the declines.

This author entered financial markets in the 1970s when the ordinary stockbroker typically advised that gold should be 5% of a portfolio.

This number is still given out today by investment advisors.

Isn't it interesting that your investment advisor will allow 5% of your holdings to be in gold but the ECB insists on 20% of gold for its own holdings?

Yes, gold just like currencies has been "digitized." Paper gold was created for the trade of oil.

Another, January 17, 1998

Our new thinking today sees digitized paper gold as a diversion of investment away from physical gold, as a strategy to keep the price down by scattering gold interest into non-gold or synthetic gold instruments.

But here *Another* makes the historical point that the original electronic instruments representing gold or tracking gold prices made it possible to supplement oil deals with different kinds of paper contracts attractive to the sellers.

The oil seller, valuing gold, would take certain paper representing gold in addition to taking paper money payments.

Oil contracts could have these "premiums" associated with them and the "premiums" did not require physical delivery of gold while at the same time they represented gold "value" (expressed in paper currency).

The oil seller could feel he was getting cash plus gold for oil. He was probably getting cash plus cash, depending on how the contracts were redeemed.

The supplemental value of these apparently "non-cash" contracts kept the market price of oil lower since one part of the deal was transparent (marked to PUBLIC markets) and the premium part of the deal was private.

It's natural to ask if, with all of the of paper gold in the markets today, if the use of paper gold has spread to other kinds of supplemental dealmaking.

In the future, many "salesmen of leverage" will tell stories of the fact that could not be. "The demand for gold "the “element" will vanish, as the dollar price for "gold the money" does soar".

Another, August 19, 1998

The “salesmen of leverage” manage gold as a commodity like pork bellies. They may offset gold exposure with some other trade. They may sell gold short, write options, and so on.

A separation of the gold and paper gold markets will occur when the price of physical gold is set, not by paper traders, but by large scale physical transactions.

The anonymous blogger FOFOA explains it this way: “The new gold market will be physical only and the price will be set by physical transactions at the top level at which it flows!!” He notes, “Traders that believe gold is overvalued at $55k or whatever will have no say in the matter. They won’t be able to short it and buy up their favorite correlated commodity anymore ... gold will no longer be a commodity.”

“Salesmen of leverage” will be baffled as gold, the element, disappears into trade among giants.

[O]ne must see the mining companies for what they "do," not what they "are." These companies are in business not to make "gold", but to make "profits" in terms of currencies!

Another, June 14, 1998

This much has not changed since 1998: too many goldbugs still value mining stocks for their gold in the ground. Too many value them as proxies for gold.

They are businesses to make currency not gold. Some have bad management, some will make bad decisions in the future, some have excessive debt, some made false or unrealistic surveys, some will be taken over by conglomerates with other priorities.

Mining companies have all the foibles of companies, especially indebted companies.

One of the most famous blunders of the mining company stock analysts was to project out of the 1970s and 1980s an increased pace in the advance of extraction technology. The gold production increases they foresaw did not happen. Perhaps a new wave of engineering innovation is around the corner. Perhaps not.

As this is written, gold mining companies are the worst-performing sector of the stock market. In other words, among paper trades, they are especially bad.

Even if they were doing well, companies remain companies and gold remains gold.

Days pass easily as a thousand years of history give backing to our investment. "For what I hold is not an empty promise. Nor is it a major thought of debt. I am now today, paid in full!"

Another, November 07, 1997

It may help to break this into pieces.

"Days pass easily as a thousand years of history give backing to our investment."

We are not following the day-to-day gold/currency price movements in the markets. Gold will be worth gold when needed. History proves it.

"For what I hold is not an empty promise."

I hold gold. I do not hold a contract for future delivery of gold. I do not hold a stock certificate representing gold collectively managed in a vault. I do not carry some sort of IOU for gold. I hold gold.

"**Nor is it a major thought of debt."**

My gold is not a promise to pay in full. It is not backed by the full faith and credit of this or that government. It is not revalued as currency on currency markets by the thoughts of others, from moment to moment.

"I am now today, paid in full!"

The transaction is complete. Gold has no counterparty to fail, no coupon to redeem, no "full faith and credit" to prop up its value. It is not a debt instrument, it has no maturity date, and it cannot expire worthless.

Gold extinguishes the debt, closes the transaction. Currency cannot do that.

But I say, spend your time in the company of truly wealthy ones, see how they make gold lie very still!

Another, February 7, 1998

What does it mean to make gold lie very still?

The Wall Street term on everybody's lips in recent years is "re-hypothecating."

The truly wealthy ones do not "re-hypothecate" their gold. They do not lend it out at interest, sell option contracts on their gold, or otherwise disturb their own titles to this property. It is off the market and out of sight. It does nothing but be gold.

How still might gold lie?

So still that no one even knows you have it.

Know this now, the world will again, in your time, feel value in gold as never before. And that value will be as the "productive use of holding wealth thru the fire of change. "Yes, you can also walk in the footsteps of giants."

Another, February 7, 1998

We have in our time, as *Another* predicted, begun to feel the value of gold as never before. The value has very much been one of surviving the fire of change and with the greatest changes yet to come, the fire's heat will increase.

The common stockbroker continues to suggest a 5% gold holding in one's portfolio as a hedge. Those seeing or feeling the fires of change will not be satisfied with this.

When *Another* says that we can walk in the footsteps of giants he means that we too can accumulate gold like the "truly wealthy ones" as long as the markets remain open and as long as the price is suppressed to allow accumulation at low cost.

We will not be able to walk in the footsteps of giants when gold is no longer priced in currency, when paper burns, and when there are many bids but no asks.

Buy physical gold and hold it close. Real wealth cannot know time, it is good for all seasons. It will buy you honor during a time without truth!

Another, February 5, 1998

How can gold by honor? What is a *time without truth*?

A *time without truth* is a time when currency lies about its value, when it cannot deliver on its function as a fair or honest medium of exchange.

Honor depends on fair exchange and there will come a time when paper money cannot facilitate a fair exchange. In that time, men will depend on gold to make honorable transactions.

False wealth, currency, is a prisoner of time.

What did the markets say the value of a dollar was today? What do currency options say a dollar will be worth in 60 days? Time will tell.

Real wealth, gold, is timeless.

Holding it close means holding it within reach. Keeping it accessible.

"Physical gold" has become a byword among gold buyers since 1998 but not enough buyers have considered "holding it close."

A receipt for gold in a vault controlled by others is not "holding it close."

For as persons need real things for life, they do "want" and "reach" for a "real measure for worth".

Another, February 22, 1998

People naturally want nourishment, a roof overhead, clothing, a measure of security.

Financially, they want a "real measure for worth." Outside of the West, this means gold and jewelry. In the West, this means dollars or euros.

"Sound as a dollar." This misleading idea is spread by every level of schooling in the West and confuses the natural tendency for people to reach for real worth.

It is not completely successful. Westerners still buy art and the art market can be said to be driven not by art lovers but by people of means seeking "real measure of worth." They are storing future value.

There is a similar situation in classic cars, in choice real estate, in many types of "collectibles." These collectibles markets are driven not by collectors per se but by those reaching for "real measure of worth."

However well these may substitute for gold, gold remains the 'real measure of worth."

Political, legal and military "currencies" do come and go with the "seasons", but "gold currency" did keep promise for citizens of changing times!

Another, April 26, 1998

The permanence of gold as currency emerges in every new "season" of political change or military occupation.

Whenever military scrip is issued by an occupier, we can be sure that gold is the preferred medium of exchange.

Has the government issued a "new lira" to replace the "old lira"? Gold will also change hands and will be the preferred currency.

And in any season of political change, does the one receiving gold in a transaction regret it? Feel cheated?

Gold always keeps its promises.

You will find a new financial future in a value from the past. The world will embrace gold as "a better inheritance for our children" for it has now become a "lifetime holding".

Another, April 26, 1998

Current events have made this note ironic.

Our current fiscal-financial-monetary crises are of such long duration that even if you intended to hold gold only for the length of our troubles, it would become a “lifetime holding” considering the pace at which events are playing out.

But this “metal from the past” imposes the longer view on us.

It’s not just a question of judging our current troubles as an exceptional state. These are the cycles of history and if things were calm now, your children could reasonably expect worse.

Wealth stored as gold can deliver a new financial future. It can be held for multiple lifetimes. It is the better inheritance than fiat.

... [E]veryone knows that western minds don't like or want gold, but if they think you like it they will trade it up in price for the sake of "sticking it to you".

Another, January 17, 1998

Here, *Another* was commenting on trading patterns and a quirk of market psychology.

At the point that it becomes a "given" that non-Western gold accumulation has started in earnest, market games will be played in order to make money on the interest in gold shown by others.

The trader mind is about making profits. A non-Western interest in gold presents an opportunity for gain.

The market's players will not be interested in *why* non-Westerners want gold and they themselves will not want it. The game will be to make money off of a buying trend by others.

This will help explain an active market where that market does not understand or appreciate what it is trading.

The Western governments needed to keep the price of gold down so it could flow where they needed it to flow. The key to free up gold was simple. The Western public will not hold an asset that going nowhere, at least in currency terms.

Another, November 21, 1997

The Western public wants returns. No returns, less buying of that asset. Less buying, lower price.

One of the scenarios that gold investors like to talk about is one in which the Western public suddenly desires gold. They imagine what their gold holdings will be when the Western public wakes up. (Of course, this reveals a trader's mind, not the mind of a wealth accumulator.)

Gold ownership becomes a "loser" in the West by ensuring gold is a "non-performing" asset. This means that if the price of gold is stable, gold owners will sell to invest money in more "rewarding" investments that appreciate in value, pay dividends, etc. If gold can be seen to decline in dollar price over time, even better.

If the public scorns gold as non-performing, there is more gold in the market to flow "where needed." At the time of writing, *Another* noted that gold was needed to supplement oil contracts.

The problem of keeping gold "going nowhere" has been a struggle for Western governments. As documented on the GATA website, a wide variety of central bank techniques have been used to keep the price down, to keep gold underperforming.

Current thinking is that the distortions in gold markets are culminating in events that will force a price rise.

Time will tell.

09. Silver

Silver will always be part of "gold money." But, [it] is far too small a market for large, modern economies. Silver will do far better than any paper asset, only it will serve better as a "personal holding" than as a major money. If it is of your way to balance wealth, then silver will show value.

Another, January 23, 1998

A quick reading of this note suggests *Another* is talking about metal-backed currency. However, it is a statement about wealth.

Silver owners may remember "silver certificates" and silver coins. In those days, silver acted as a medium of exchange with a wealth component. In that sense it was money, the same way gold is money.

As a currency backing, both silver and gold are infinitely divisible. But as a wealth holding, they are not because one must have the physical in hand. There is not enough silver in the world to store the wealth of the many.

What chance would the tiny silver supply have to fill every hand or pocket in the world?

Another here says there is not enough silver in existence or in production to form the wealth of "large, modern economies." Silver owners with their "personal holdings" are well positioned to transact small business and make modest collections that will "show value" in time.

Silver, in short supply, is a reasonable personal holding.

Gold, in much larger supply, is a holding for nations, "giants," and intergenerational wealth.

Silver is good, but always too small.

Another, February 4, 1998

Another saw, or was party to, very large (private) gold transactions. Then and in our day these transactions were based in dollars.

In considering the dollar values represented by the volumes of gold involved, these large deals could not be conducted in silver. There is not enough silver to match the dollar values underlying the largest physical gold transactions.

In recent times, a shortage of deliverable physical silver developed. It became difficult to take delivery of silver in settling futures contracts, for instance. Many months later, the same situation developed in the much larger gold market.

Silver preceded gold in this shortage.

Now, the trader mind looks at the small size of the silver market and sees shortages and sees opportunities for making a good pile of fiat.

Another was not looking at silver with the trader mind but with the intention of storing wealth.

For that, on the scale of the "giants," silver is too small.

Think of the saying, "Silver is the common man's gold."

In future currency wars, silver will show a return, but it may prove as uncertain as the economy?

Another, June 14, 1998

The commentators in precious metals warn us about the volatility of silver priced in dollars. For the trader mind, here is risk and reward.

These pundits have another favorite point: gold and silver follow entirely different dynamics. They will tell us that silver is consumed (used up); its supply is small and variable; that it is not stored or accumulated by central banks; that different industries use silver for this or that.

Some commentators complain of silver market manipulation. A small market, however, is more easily corrupted than a larger one.

These and other factors make silver volatile. But consider also the smallholders who collect silver.

If silver is a small holding grasped by "weak hands" it will enter and leave the market as economic conditions change and as its owners require currency.

Silver stores wealth for that "rainy day." "Rainy days" affect the supply of silver on the market (along some of the other factors mentioned).

Uncertainty must be considered when accumulating silver for long-term wealth.

Remember, you buy "silver for purpose" but "trade currency for gold for conclusion".

Another, June 14, 1998

What is the “purpose” of silver? It stores wealth for a rainy day, upon which day it is traded; or it it provides profit and loss in trading; or it temporarily hedges something.

What is the “conclusion?” It is the conclusion of wealth, the place where money lies still. It is the store of value that will never be redeemed or it will be redeemed in a distant future by a generation afar from us.

Silver could be bought “for conclusion” but rarely is. It represents a temporary storage place for our money.

One kind of silver collector is constantly repricing silver in currency and dreaming of the day when he can unload that silver for a healthy “profit” in paper. That silver serves one kind of purpose.

Another kind of collector has silver to use as currency - a medium of exchange - in case of an economic crisis. That silver has a purpose.

Some silver bug wishes to own gold but cannot afford steady buying of ounces or other standard units. Silver is a proxy for gold and may eventually be converted into gold, in this case serving that purpose.

Finally, there is the smallholder who may see silver as a better store of wealth than currency but who has day-to-day needs and therefore “weak hands.” Bad times will claim this wealth sooner rather than later. It will have served its purpose.

Silver does not lead to a conclusion.

10. Governments

Without real physical [gold] to supply the oil states, they WILL bid for gold with oil! The BIS will do the only thing they can, halt all trading and declare gold a "world oil currency"! To that end, all forms of paper gold will burn. How long till this starts?

Another, November 28, 1997

Half of this scenario is now unfolding as certain pariah oil states drop out of the dollar market and begin doing deals for gold.

As this is written, gold for oil is being exchanged between India and Iran and Afghanistan appears to be supplying a market (or venue) for broader Iranian oil-for-gold trade.

Other states, such as China and Russia, have negotiated direct oil deals that may or may not involve gold.

Imagine that this initial gold-based trade starts to dry up gold availability. Gold stops flowing where it is needed (to oil states) and so to get gold, oil states in good standing have to act like pariah oil states and bypass the dollar offering oil for gold.

What part does the Bank for International Settlements (BIS) play in this? The BIS is the central bank (CB) for central bankers and handles their inter-CB gold deals. The BIS would "halt all trading" to stabilize the gold supply and get it flowing where it needs to flow.

A student of *Another*, the blogger FOFOA, proposes a different outcome. He suggests that the BIS might reprice gold to get it flowing again. They could do this by, for example, offering to buy at (say) $55,000 an ounce and sell at $56,000 an ounce. Dealers would buy below $55k/oz and pocket the difference.

Whatever the merits of this scenario, the BIS reprice would have to account for the value of oil in gold.

The major threat to this collection of [paper] wealth holdings would be the introduction of any real asset currency. Any country that could "resource a currency" of use the world over [i.e. gold or oil] does pose a threat to the wealth of nations greater then war!

Another, February 7, 1998

This comment envisions a scenario in roughly these three parts:

(1) A government announces its currency will be fully or partially backed by gold, silver, oil or some commodity.

(2) There is an immediate worldwide "flight to quality" as people quickly shift their fiat and assets to the new currency.

(3) The shift drains current investments while flooding markets with unbacked currencies (worthless fiat).

All this would happen faster than governments could react, thus collapsing currency values, paper trading venues, paper holdings denominated in fiat, and it would (at least temporarily) halt supply chains, global trade, and myriad smaller transactions.

Often market crises happen overnight and faster than anyone can react. The market closes at one level and opens at some other.

This potential disruption is the basis for saying such action is a threat greater than war; its effects would be more devastating than what a war could achieve.

Among the ideas now circulating, one says that selected U.S. military interventions and sanction regimens are linked to a plan to maintain the U.S. dollar as the world's reserve currency. This is achieved by preventing certain states from leaving the dollar trading arena and through occupations that enlarge the dollar transaction realm.

This theory represents a flip side of *Another's* observation above.

There are nations that will try to "resource a new currency" as the old financial system implodes. Oil or gold or both may be used. If it is done at the correct time, much will be gained by all! Fail this attempt, and gold will never trade on an open exchange again in our lifetime!

Another, February 14, 1998

The weakening of global financial arrangements, especially any decline in the use of dollars in trade, will tempt some states into "front running" the next international financial system. As *Another* suggests in his previous comment, the surest escape hatch from the current system into a future system would be to back a currency with something.

The backing of a new currency would have such immediate and devastating effects on other currencies (especially in foreign trade) that it would be tantamount to war.

However, *Another* says it is possible to time the introduction such that all would gain. One imagines that to be a situation where fiat currencies have collapsed or devalued on their own to the point that markets are already frozen or wrecked and everyone is waiting for a saving recourse. This would be an orderly exit from ruin and it is possible to imagine gold continuing to trade and to be available.

If, however, the system collapses from the sudden impetus of a gold standard adoption, the demand for gold would become such that there would be many bids but no asks ... for the duration of a lifetime.

Further, there is great risk that gold would be nationalized as a common asset belonging to the people.

In the same way that all oil in the Middle East (and most other major producing countries) is nationally owned for the good of all, gold in the ground will be deemed a "currency reserve" for the good of all.

Another, December 16, 1997

Should gold become the basis of a currency, there would be great impetus to nationalize all gold and gold mines.

In the U.S., there have been a number of efforts in history to nationalize mining on federal lands.

The private ownership of gold would have to persist in secret and the output of all mines would go to the state.

If energy is a national asset, certainly minerals will be labeled a national treasure that belongs to all the people. This would fit well with a scenario where gold is needed by the mint or treasury.

When any commodity becomes money, the free market is not allowed to produce such without laws to govern that production.

Another, April 5, 1998

Just as gold has been banished from money theory, the related idea has taken root that government owns our money; that money is a function of government; that the supply of money is the government's business; and that uncontrolled money is a curse that ruins nations through inflation, booms, busts, and vicious cycles.

Most readers will know that the money function of the old royal mints was to stamp money out of gold and silver brought there by private persons. The king took a piece of that as seigneurage.

The roles are now reversed. The government brings its raw paper money to market and the market puts a currency exchange value on the government's money.

In the United States, the comparison is even closer. The Federal Reserve "mints" paper dollars and these are distributed in instruments that pass through the hands of private bankers who take *their* seigneurage out in the form of interest.

Should gold become money, the modern government will not be confounded by miners producing their own money out of the ground.

Governments will tax mines for the right to produce money and force them to sell production in terms of "whatever the new world reserve currency" is at that time. Euro? Because gold mines are the "unique" circumstance in world of investments, their owners will suffer a "unique" problem of defining what they really own!

Another, September 3, 1998

Another sees what could be called a fascist economic outcome in which production remains in private (favored) hands but terms of production, supply, and cost are set by the state.

However, we have to be ready for a communist outcome as well in which the state seizes and operates mines itself.

In either case *Another* notes that all pricing will be in currency (the world reserve currency) rather than gold.

Note that with state control, currency is not priced against gold but gold against currency! This raises the existential question of *what is it that is being mined*? Currency?

What is it that mine owners own? A currency production facility? Or as today, a system for earning fiat?

This high strangeness is a function of the mispricing of currency and gold.

Today, no nation/currency is on a gold standard. The first country that starts will own the rest for some time.

Another, February 4, 1998

The adoption of a gold standard would create an immediate rush out of fiat currencies into the new gold money. There would be a flight to value. Central banks would need to replace their reserves quickly.

Holders of fiat would see the value drop dramatically as it was sold off for gold or the new gold-backed money.

Governments that continued to try to buy and sell in the old paper currency would be subject to arbitrage, with the conversion rate between real money and fiat being so large that immense amounts of fiat would be at the disposal of gold (or gold money) owners.

This would disrupt "orderly" markets by making everything priced in fiat "cheap" to gold money owners. It would allow gold money to buy real property, companies, and resources for "peanuts" in the resulting disparity in currency values.

The immediate offset to foreign adoption of a gold standard might look like classic inflation; one might see a Zimbabwe effect where a normal unit of exchange becomes a trillion dollars or such.

The unwieldiness of such fiat, its declining value, and the government's helplessness in the face of these forces will break the public's confidence sooner rather than later.

Meanwhile, holders of gold money will "own the rest."

I prepare for not the war of men, but the war of currencies! This conflict will bring forth a new concept for many: "western governments will encourage people to hold physical gold "!

Another, September 3, 1998

China watchers have noticed that the government has encouraged private gold ownership. Meanwhile, the Bank of Japan is aggressively devaluing its currency to increase exports.

The world is convinced that cheapening the dollar is one motive behind the Federal Reserve flooding the world with easy dollar credits and dollars. James Rickards has written a book explaining that we are in a currency war.

How is the currency war connected to private gold ownership?

As mentioned earlier, the currency war will end when one government or another announces a gold or commodity backing for its money. The first mover will have an immediate and devastating effect on all fiat that will impoverish anyone holding fiat.

Those private persons holding gold will escape some of the effects of the sudden appearance of a gold or oil backed currency.

Even if a gold or commodity backed currency were introduced slowly and in an orderly fashion (one struggles to imagine how that could happen), those holding gold would benefit in the sense that the new currency would have been "pre-distributed" into their hands.

Their wealth rests at a destination to which other wealth is still traveling.

What country would have the brilliant wisdom and daring to make gold its currency and thus own the world? What new regional entity, yet to form, could accomplish this?

Another, February 7, 1998

At the time this was written, it appeared to some that the European Union might be the regional entity to accomplish this because of the way its Euro was configured (it was more of an accounting unit than a dollar-type fiat) and because of the European Central Bank's commitment to gold reserves as backing for the new Euro.

These hopes were misplaced, however.

Now, rather than an act of wisdom and daring, the adoption of gold as currency seems to be a function of international economic boycotts. The Iranians are under a strict trade boycott and their banking is restricted abroad. So too, the North Koreans.

This is causing a reversion to barter and to gold based transactions.

We do see movement in Latin America towards creation of a regional currency with a pan-national bank to be headquartered in Caracas. We see the formation of APEC, a trade bloc formed by the Shanghai accord. Commentator Jim Willie sees this as a group moving towards a gold currency.

The effects of adopting a gold standard would be so sudden and so devastating to the world that while the adopter would reap immense benefits, the losers could regard the move as an act of war.

Even the initial steps towards such an adoption could trigger a violent overreaction. A recent book, *Petrodollar Warfare*, proposes that certain U.S. military conflicts have to do with threats to the dollar standard. Even if this is overstated, the argument has real potential.

The other regional entities moving away from dollars and potentially towards gold are the BRIC countries, China and Russia especially, and the Gulf states.

Governments must return to gold or they will perish. It is only a matter of time.

Another, April 18, 1998

In gold circles today, it is widely said that the world is in the midst of the longest experiment in history with pure fiat currency and that there is no precedent for this ending well (since all individual fiat trials ended in chaos).

Governments are incentivized to cheapen the value of their currencies in order to promote exports and "economic growth." Governments are also operating their fiat currencies through the medium of modern fractional reserve banking, a house of cards that not only promotes cyclical instability but also enriches a small, favored class of bankers at the expense of widows, orphans, pensioners, and anyone on fixed incomes.

In other words, fiat weakens social and political stability over time while destroying the economic foundations of the underlying society.

That governments will perish is inevitable. How they perish may be tragic.

It is today, treasuries only can print currency, so will it be tomorrow that only government[s] buy and give citizens real money, gold!

Another, April 19, 1998

Here, *Another* is looking forward to the day when money is based on gold and the government has nationalized the production of gold.

The the circulation of gold money thus would begin with state ownership of gold in the ground. Mined and minted, it would enter the economy through government transactions, including payment for goods and services, payment of civil servants, and so on.

This is the path through which the U.S. attempted to circulate dollar coins, but the coins are shunned.

The government will buy gold on the market or through a cost of production. It will give gold by settling its affairs in that medium or through a medium backed by gold.

If you hold your value in a public way, it will be taxed or taken for the good of all.

Another, November 23, 1997

This is equally true for publicly perceived wealth and for the private means of gold production.

Gold held in a public way will be taken to serve the "public good."

That does not mean the government has lost interest in private wealth. Remember government persecution of "hoarders" throughout history. Whenever shortages are perceived, "speculators" and "hoarders" are declared to be public enemies.

Wealth held "in a public way," however, will attract the government's interest first.

The large modern currencies, of today have only debt ridden economies to back them. They cannot change as debt blocks their path. "To change is to live and to live, some debts must die".

Another, February 4, 1998

The truth that "some debts must die" has been felt sharply after the crisis of 2008, when government intervened to prevent debts from dying anywhere, ever.

This truth is felt by students who must live but whose debts are of a special type, protected by law from ever dying.

Furthermore, again using today's headlines, many of the leading economies have a debt-to-GDP ratio of over 100%. In other words, they have borrowed more than they produce in any given year.

Their debts act as constraints on many different potential policies.

Economic reform must always consider the status of the creditor. Moreover, creditors have different identities which translate into different roles. There is the foreign creditor of a rival government; there is the domestic creditor who is a leading bank with a major role in the issuance of money and new debt. There is the proverbial widow pensioner. There is the retirement fund of the civil service.

Debt management could potentially cripple policymaking with such complexity in play. Economic management has little wiggle room in a space wholly occupied by debt management.

Worthless paper currencies are now used in every country of the world. There is no safe place to save. Thus there can be no capital and no capitalism. It is only a matter of time.

Another, Sat Apr 18 1998

Paper currencies are instruments of capital destruction. The mispricing of everything by fiat money results in malinvestment. Malinvestment produces both capital droughts in some areas of the economy while floods of capital wash through other parts of the economy.

Great savings held in paper money puts those savings at the mercy of financial policies.

In America at this moment, the banks are stocked with cash they will not lend. They invest it in a tower-of-Babylon stock market; they use it to buy assets and risk it in trading and speculation. A great deal of it, they leave sitting in their own accounts at the central bank.

There is no certainty whether currency holdings will maintain their value (as countries race to devalue their currencies). There is no incentive to save as the government pays zero percent interest to "encourage" home ownership and keep down the cost of its own borrowing.

There can be no certainty that currency savings will hold value as debts balloon and as the state borrows more money to dispense subsidies to favored supporters.

I think the governments will change the rules, just before you decide to sell [gold stocks]. It is the way of life, yes? Is it not the "human nature" to rob the bank with the most money?

Another, April 18, 1998

Here, *Another* responded to a question that asked why wouldn't the owners of gold mines profit immensely with the adoption of a gold standard.

When gold becomes that important, it will be seized, or its production regulated, or its selling price set in such a way as to benefit the government at the expense of owners.

Unless the owners of gold mines were such politically important persons that they could not be trifled with, the exchange would be set in favor of the state.

More important is the question, "It is the way of life, yes?"

There is a tendency among investors to believe that contracts will be honored, that guarantees are enforceable in court, that the counterparty will always be there, and so on.

This is called continuity bias. The Great Depression generation followed something different, call it the uncertainty principle.

It is the way of life that in fact nothing is certain and that the strong take from the weak. That is what makes the protection of gold (not gold mines or gold claims) so important.

The government is always going to go where the money is and it arrives with no intent to honor contracts and pre-existing arrangements.

The government will always go the "the bank with the most money" to meet its costs and pursue its aims.

Neither myself nor any other person should enrich their home by holding the assets that give "bondage upon future life"

Another, April 4, 1998

The very oddest thing about an American dollar is that it begins as a debt instrument. Ellen Brown has written, "Federal Reserve Notes (dollar bills) are issued by the Federal Reserve, a *private* banking corporation, and *lent* to the government."

It helps to understand that the dollar is a government bond without a coupon, one that pays no interest.

Elsewhere *Another* had noted that the dollar, the world's reserve currency, "was supplied as debt, borrowed from the future of children yet unborn."

But the dollar is not the end of the story. Investors tend to hold dollars not as cash but as Treasury obligations: bonds, bills, notes.

Holding a Treasury is a bondage upon taxpayers. The note or bill holder is a creditor of the taxpayer's government. If the debts of that government are large enough that they cannot be paid out of normal income, they become "bondage upon future life."

This is expressed by some today in the political discourse as indebting our children.

We do now reach high production of goods and service worldwide. But, in terms of our financial system, the ability to trade these goods, has reached its limit!

The economy has reached "the top of the mountain" and no one can see this.

Another, February 14, 1998

Once oil came to be traded with a gold supplement, this signaled a fatal weakness in the dollar as the international medium for trade settlement. It meant that the dollar was not completely satisfactory on its own.

Trade is especially hindered in and with states that have limited access to dollars.

Today, many bilateral trade settlement arrangements are being tried, the most common being a currency swap arrangement. None of these has proved compelling enough to replace the dollar. Experiments continue.

Another believed that these experiments, which began at the time he was writing, would resolve into a partial or total gold standard for trade settlement.

Where gold is used to settle trade, it acts as a regulator over trade: no gold, no buying power.

In the states, US dollars can be printed to buy as much production from the world as expanding credit permits. Imports are unlimited by the need to earn gold to buy goods and thus, world production is maximized.

This is the top of the mountain: dollars representing credits are used to purchase manufactures, stimulating manufacture beyond our ability to trade them without further damaging the dollar, the medium of trade settlement.

More simply, owning the world's reserve currency has given the US unlimited buying power. Unlimited buying has stimulated high production. This is the top of the mountain.

The last twenty years of transition do not represent the future of this world class money.

Another, June 14, 1998

Here, *Another* refers to the history of gold, 1978-1998. He correctly sees this period as full of anomalies.

- 1978 - Gold reaches $195/oz in July as USA inflation skyrockets.
- 1979 - Gold reaches $300 in July as Paul Volcker appointed Federal Reserve Chairman.
- 1980 - Gold reaches $850 in January as Volcker begins dollar rescue.
- 1981 - U.S. prime lending rate remains at 20%, causing a rush of dollars out of gold into credit.
- 1982 - As rates are brought down, dollars leave credit for the stock market and gold.
- 1983 - Gold reaches $510 in January, then declines into the $300s and stagnation.
- 1983-1998 - The stock market boom acts as a capital magnet and gold prices enter 15 years of sideways movement.

A large part of this transition happened outside of publicly traded gold prices. This is the massive expansion of dollar debt obligations by the USA and the long period of dollar debasement.

One might also say it is capped by the beginning of a currency war intensified by the movement toward a Euro currency.

During our journey in life, it will be the "world events" that truly "fill in the blanks" as this "economic drama" unfolds!

Another, August 11, 1998

The humility of *Another* is not feigned. He came to an open forum to share what he knew and what he thought. But unlike the economists or pundits, he did not fill in the whole canvas with his own colors.

He believed certain outcomes were inevitable because he saw and worked with "giants" who were shaping outcomes.

At the same time, he saw gaps in the story that could not be filled by extrapolation, inference, or "best judgment."

What those gaps might be go beyond the scope of this book but the reader can be sure of one thing. The divulgence of the facts behind *Another's* thinking do not give us a full account of what is happening and what might happen.

Moreover, he likely did not even share all of his facts with us.

What *Another* gave us was the picture of a hidden dynamic that was at work; of forces tending toward predictable outcomes; he named the counterforces known to him and their desired outcomes; and he treated timelines somewhat vaguely, leaving room for "world events" to fill in those blanks.

Most importantly, and hardest for us to understand as Westerners, is that his timeframes were intergenerational. We may not even live to see those world events

10. Gold Hoarding

Gold has always been funny in that way. So many people worldwide think of it as money, it tends to dry up as the price rises.

Another, October 5, 1997

As Westerners, it is not asking too much of us to think of gold as a store of value. After all, we can regard paintings as stores of value, so too with stamp collections, real estate, etc.

Now, the idea of a "store of value" is (obviously) to store value. If it is surplus above our needs, we are going to store it. Gold holds value and may be stored. This much is easy for our Western culture to understand.

The part we have difficulty with is gold-as-money. If the dollar price of gold is rising, we want to "cash in," we want to "score" a big gain in fiat. This is because gold to us is an object or commodity and currency is money.

Thought experiment: what if gold was money? If you think of gold as money, the proposition changes as the dollar price of gold rises. As the dollar value increases, the questions become, "Why do I want to change my gold money into this paper? What would be the correct paper currency value for this gold since the paper money cannot store value?"

This is why, as the gold price in currency rises, the trading supply dries up. The higher the rise, the sharper the rise, the more difficult the answer to those two questions.

The Paper Gold Market today could completely destroy the physical market by shutting down all possible trading as the currencies are devalued by gold in a massive upheaval!

Another, January 23, 1998

The paper market follows its own rules and its own dynamic. Events in the paper market could cause the withdrawal of physical gold from circulation.

At the present time, for example, there are severe shortages of physical gold for contract delivery and some analysts are expecting this to ultimately "shut down all possible trading."

But *Another* links this to a specific event, namely "as the currencies are devalued by gold." Imagine:

- Currencies are devalued against gold by central banks or by some other event
- The move is sudden, a "massive upheaval"
- The paper gold market has to reflect gold vs. fiat pricing immediately
- The upheaval wipes out contracts and destroys paper gold customers; the alternative is that the market shuts down to adjust
- The paper market benchmark price for gold, being unavailable, takes physical sellers off the public markets

Some analysts have noted that hyperinflation is an overnight event. This applies to currency revaluations generally. Has there ever been a slow, orderly revaluation?

These revaluations shut down all markets, at least temporarily, and gold would be similarly affected.

11. Musings

The concept of what wealth is is going to change.

Another, January 11, 1998

This comment is for those who think wealth is income. This is widespread among Americans, in particular, with an entire taxation system built around the notion that income equals wealth. In the USA, "the wealthy" are always high earners.

In the world of *Another*, and the world at large, high income earners are the hirelings of the wealthy. They are the managers, caretakers and stewards of various assets. Commonly, high income people do not even have contact with the wealthy. The idea that high income earners are wealthy distracts attention from where it is not wanted.

Now, the wealthy are not such by virtue of hoarding fiat, which has no stable value and limited intergenerational potential. The wealthy have a different idea of value.

So when crises comes, the wealthy remain wealthy and their high income servants return to the general workforce.

There is a second side to this comment. It is for those who think wealth is investment. Recall *Another's* observation that money moves *through* investments. Having bought a stock or other financial instrument, your money has gone elsewhere and you are holding an obligation, or contract, or receipt. These are not wealth.

Finally, a third aspect to *Another's* remark. If you ask yourself, "Where is real value," and you answer land or diamonds or income streams, you are still denominating value in dollars (or other currency). You are trying to calibrate stored value in a medium of exchange, which is impossible.

In the past, everything was priced in gold, including currency. The link remains but is unclear. This is why the concept of wealth must change.

Time will prove all things!

Another, March 7, 1998

Time is the test of theories and predictions and *Another* is happy to subject himself to this. He does this not with the false humility of the public prophet who expects vindication but as the student of history who expects to be corrected in part or full.

Considering the whole body of his writing, we see Another humbly proposing outcomes to events he was personally involved in. He observed markets, he acted in those markets (for "giants"), he saw the effects of his actions reflected in those markets, and he gained insights into developments playing out behind curtains of secrecy.

He had the additional advantage of a "non-Western mind" which allowed him to more easily access the traditional purposes of gold.

In subjecting his views to the tests of time, *Another* is allowing room not only for interpretation but repudiation.

He offers his *Thoughts* as propositions.

"Your life passes, thoughts change and a person's perception of value does mature....it is the way of people, some are part of the future, as they become the history of the past"

Another, April 26, 1998

And so, as financial events focus us on the meaning of value, life events also force us to consider the meaning of intergenerational wealth.

We old fiat handlers, moving into gold, have reached new conclusions that are "part of the future." The future may regard us with curiosity, asking how we lived in an age of currency without money.

In considering *Another* himself, 1998 is now the past but his ideas remain part of a future to which may yet come to pass.

Perhaps this war of "money" is not located on the fixed ground of past thought, but will be waged in the fluid minds of men as they seek to defend their life's savings.

Another, August 11, 1998

As an aging population consults its estate lawyers, as "targeted inflation" erodes savings, as zero interest rate policies destroy capital, the struggle to understand the meaning of "money" comes home to many who have lived their whole lives in a paper world.

"The fixed ground of past thought," the economics teachings, the punditry, the common wisdom all begin to fade as we face the new reality of currency wars, a collapsing dollar, a failed economy, and a reallocation of our life's savings to others.

Gold in both hands lives by no rules of man, as does the business of trading nations.

Another, August 11, 1998

"The business of trading nations" lives by the rules of man. It lives by contract, law, courts, and conventions.

"Gold in both hands"—gold held firmly—follows certain timeless and stateless strictures, outside the rules of committees, states, banks, presidents, and economists.

Gold endures freely, complete in itself, dependent on nothing.

...each person must sail their own ship. My allocation is not your allocation, plan as your thoughts will allow.

Another, February 24, 1998

In making this remark, *Another* was speaking to a forum of gold collectors and gold traders. Both would naturally want to know "how much is enough." And this is where trouble begins.

Another is gauging his allocation against his ability to save (surplus over income) and his intergenerational transfer goals. His questioners are pricing gold in dollars and wondering either:

1. How to best offset dollar value losses with gold or
2. How to score lots of fiat when they sell all their gold

Anyone can understand "My allocation is not your allocation." What is much harder is "as your thoughts allow."

So many people in gold forums have thoughts that do not allow gold its correct place in their world. For instance, if you value gold in dollars, your thoughts will allow one kind of allocation.

- If you value gold in gold, your allocation will be different.
- If you have children, your allocation may be affected.
- If you have low living expenses, your allocation may be affected.

The key idea begins with, *How do you value gold*? What do your thoughts allow?

As in all things of life, it is more safe to follow a well walked trail. Truly, many have walked this path of gold. But, as no two men can take the same step, each must gather wealth as his experience will allow.

Another, March 7, 1998

Here, the "well walked trail" is this "path of gold."

Life experience allows accumulation at different rates and in different amounts, certainly at different times and in different venues.

As *Another* said, my allocation is not your allocation.

I may need cash, I may have expenses, I may be in no position today to place wealth in its "final resting place."

Is your currency still working capital? It may not be ready for its final destination. Do you even have a next generation?

Avoid formulas, even rules of thumb.

Indeed, a fit body and strong mind will be needed to carry gold down this economic mountain! The weight of gold will cause some to fall, even as others find this load helps to place the foot firmly on ground.

Another, March 7, 1998

This is a poetic way to say that gold accumulated before the crisis or during it may not help one to transcend the crisis.

Some will sell their gold to earn inflated sums of fiat, deceived by the value behind the transaction.

Some gold owners with "weak hands" will be shaken out of their holdings by schemers, governments, shifting markets.

Some gold owners will diversify into land, contracts, or other arrangements that cost them their gold in a bad exchange.

Some, however, may use their gold to reach a safe and secure place. The strong mind will keep its gold focus and the fit body will apply "strong hands" to keeping the gold in a strong grasp until descending the mountain.

Times of chaos are just that, with confusion rampant and emotions running strong. In those times, gold will pass from weak hands to strong.

Risk not your wealth in paper, we enter a period of truth.

Another, January 10, 1998

These times are not the times of 1997, but in 1997 people rightly viewed themselves in the midst of a fiat currency crisis that was gaining strength. The collapse they foresaw was forestalled and yet we feel as they do, that the breakdown in this experiment of "thought money" is nearing its end.

The signs *Another* mentioned are all around us. We also have new signs since his day.

This is the end of a period of lies that stretches back to the time of his writing.

Even if the defenders of fiat currency manage to hang on for another 25 years, that moment of truth will only have been deferred ... and at how much misery.

Even in this "light of day" a trader/ government will tell you, "hold not that commodity, gold, for it is as a dead, unproductive asset". I say, run from these lies, for they see not deep in the future!

Another, February 7, 1998

We live in an age of "continuity bias" where the yearning for "normal" extrapolates into thousands of identical tomorrows.

We have a steady-state mindset, we believe, religiously, in incremental change, accurate models, economic forecasts, and expert opinions from highly credentialed consensus seekers.

The appreciation of gold, in currency values, led some conventional wisdom to say "Gold should be a part of everyone's portfolio," but the amounts referred to here were near 5%.

But now, unlike *Another's* time, the warning about gold tends to be that it is a "volatile asset," that it may be "overpriced," and that it is in a price bubble that will eventually burst. Avoid gold!

But really, all this is investor talk from a trader mind.

Depending on how deep into the future we look, there is 100% certainty that there will be no dollar and 100% certainty that there will be gold.

You will find not the lies of paper in my house.

Another, March 8, 1998

Another is not "playing the market." He is not extending credits to bankrupt governments, nor is he buying paper that will make a killing at the expense of some counterparty.

He is not collecting the tax money of fellow citizens by clipping government bond coupons, nor is he feeding paper fuel into the furnace of a fractional reserve banking system.

He is doing something different, and in this difference is the whole kernel of his philosophy.

New world order, regionalism and tribalism are but modern ph[r]ases that denote "group retreat to avoid paying up".

Another, February 22 1998

Think of "tribalism" here as 20th Century "autarky," an enclosed, self-referential financial and economic system. The pre-war Hitler system modeled this idea and post-colonial states in some cases have followed suit, in Burma and North Korea for instance.

As the Axis alliances and occupations took shape, Hitler's autarky evolved into a European regionalism that relied on an exchange rate mechanism, export and import quotas set by treaties and a general extension of the autarky concept to a bloc of states. Many such regional groupings have emerged since WWII.

The "New World Order" was the watchword of the Axis powers, and the branding/marketing core of their enterprise. It was the broader framework that would integrate the various regionalisms into a "world system." "New world order" is often used without reference to the Axis ideal but in exactly the way the Axis intended.

Let us summarize what *Another* is saying in generic terms:

Tribalism. Avoids paying up by limiting exchange and settlement, by restricting money movements, imports and exports. Keeps the gold (or whatever) inside the tribe.

Regionalism. Extends the ways and means of the tribe to friends of the tribe. Restrictions keep from "paying up" outside this group. Enables some members inside the group to avoid "paying up." This is the current European crisis in a nutshell.

New world order. Combines autarkic regionalism into a "world system" in which the method of exchange is centrally managed so as to limit exchange and settlement, exports and imports, currency and credit to a highly conceptual model involving synthetic currencies, supranational central banking, centralized economic regulation and other phenomena, all of which circumvent paying up per real value.

In this time, we do stand firm with value and watch as "thoughts of others change in the wind"!

Another, February 22 1998

Think of all the discussions, all the fads associated with "safe haven investing' since 1998.

Try to read all the investing books published since 1998.

Technology investing. Real estate investing. Royalty partnerships. Make tons of currency with our proven methods.

Where is value? What is value? Some would make the answer conditional on time and circumstances.

"Stand firm with value."

Yes, we will think thoughts not spoken for simple persons.

Another, January 17, 1998

These thoughts were delivered in a gold forum at a time when gold was a simple minded proposition:

- Speculative vehicle
- Protection from inflation
- Vehicle to be converted into fiat for a big payday.

Gold fans in that forum were concerned about a number of issues:

- When should I buy and sell?
- What's the potential appreciation in dollars?
- When is my payday (in fiat)?
- What's influencing the price (in fiat)?
- What's a good mining company?
- How feasible is a gold standard?

What *Another* offered was a revolution in thinking about gold. His influence today is widespread. His ideas are considered and digested privately.

No modern gold commentator, outside of the investment field, can still operate in the 1997-98 framework. *Another's* thoughts have changed that.

Afterword: Precursors and Successors

It is worth considering the times when these ideas were published, 1997-1998, the medium, what came before and what has followed.

The quotes published in this book can be accessed at the USAGOLD website:

http://www.usagold.com/goldtrail/archives/another1.html

They represent a compilation of *Another's* posts from the KITCO forum (10/97 - 4/98), which closed, and then from the follow-on USAGOLD forum (5/98 onward). (Note that the KITCO forum was managed like a LISTSERV showing compiled emails).

Generally, this collection is considered the body of *Another's* work. It is cogent, internally cohesive, and develops thematically over time. But *Another* also posted earlier than 10/97 and those posts are in the KITCO archives:

http://bgmi.us/web/kitco/Kitco1990s.php

In May, 2012, a blogger went into the earlier KITCO archives to compile the message traffic among list subscribers whose discourse was "pre-*Another*." This very interesting traffic can be found here:

http://victorthecleaner.wordpress.com/2012/05/15/before-the-thoughts-and-before-the-trail/

This includes posts from "Big Trader," actually "The Writer" who represents "Big Trader," and *Another* himself.

Big Trader was a non-English speaker dealing in large volumes of physical gold who deputized The Writer to post his thinking to KITCO. Some of these posts were predictive of events, some were intended to correct Western thinking about gold. The Writer wrote fractured syntax with cryptic references in an oracular way:

> As a group, paper makers are very strong. But one has "cut and run"! He has come to town and wants to join us! What is this? I see other cowboys "coming down the trail"! For many years they had fun. Now a tiger chases them into town for help.

In addition to previewing the future style of *Another*, this poster's slugline occasionally appeared as *The Writer (Thoughts!)*, frontrunning *Thoughts! of Another*. It is worth noting that The Writer presented himself to KITCO readers in a similar way as *Another* would later, as a kind of consultant to a major foreign gold trading operation.

Where *Another* wrote about the bigger picture, The Writer often interested himself in market events:

> So many off market forward gold deals were done without any gold changing hands! Big buyers got on the paper side of these things and thought that the CB's were backing the dealer banks by written contract. If the mines couldn't perform the banks would ....! But what if in some deals the mines were not involved at all? Just off market option trades as backing? And some of the paper buyers shorted the futures in a big way to cover. And now whatever gold that was to back these deals is found to be "not there"? And everybody was looking at all this paper being sold and thought there must be one hell of a lot of gold being sold! Now during the last six months the price has fallen, but I have to ask, "who has got who"? (June 8, 1997)

Another (as himself) makes his first appearance in August 23, 1997:

> Hello to all!
>
> I had the opportunity to read a private reports/discussion over the last week and thought this one would have some meaning to this group. The thoughts come from a different culture and land mass so they required conversion to Western style communication. Here is from one you don't get here anymore.
>
> Why do they view their debt in terms of yield when it only returns more of the same paper? The only way to convert the return on this American debt is by buying something real with it. Only then do we have a "yield". So let us continue to view it as always before, using its pricing gage to determine value, the U.S. dollar. The marketplace is never wrong to give a high price to a low value debt as long as it uses an "unreal" currency as a value gage. The Westerners use "paper to price paper" and "more paper to price more paper" in an endless quest to add value where value only exists in the minds of men. To this end they say we have lost holding gold, but our families and children cannot go broke? No one owes us and we owe no one, and we do not "convert paper to something real" to create "yield". We already own our "yield", no conversion needed! Now they have created the illusion of gold in great supply to lower its value in currency terms, and the Americans accept this. They do not question that this illusion was done using paper contracts that do not hold gold but are priced in currencies that offer a

yield valued only in human emotion terms. It is in this fashion that the greatest folly of Western thinking will bring an end to an era of unvalued money. It will come about as the entire world evolves into those that have military might using paper currency maneuver little people countries with gold. But all gold is owned by someone, somewhere and is not free for the taking. In the near future a real value will be exchanged for gold and those that hold paper gold will bid much higher to obtain what they thought they already had!

Remember now, "a broke superpower ever destroys a simple country that has gold, they will do business with them !" —Big Trader

Now that most have converted paper gold contracts to real gold we have but to view the "great scramble" from far away. To the advantage of many, the Americans continue to position themselves in opposite fashion from the third world. They sell all real gold to hold gold contracts and gold stocks.

At some point all of the gold will be off the market. Then the CBs will be forced to become the full primary suppliers. This continued drift to CB sales will no doubt destroy most bullish gold traders until London is forced to sell real gold. Then the true volume will drive the price of gold in all currencies to such heights that it will force a reevaluation of "what was primary supply" in the first place. During this "lock up" time all Asians will be happy with the conversion price during the summer of the last few years.

Know this to be true, the millions of ounces out on hidden contracts will not be made up for by the CBs once the problem begins. During this time the new "currency price" of the entire gold stock will equal all the paper money in existence and the CBs will suddenly claim they have very little gold in an effort to hide all they can.—Big Trader

This rewrite is very close. It comes from the real one, not the fakes. Good luck!

And so here we have in a nutshell so many of the ideas that *Another* would develop over his posting career. The references to "Big Trader" suggest that *Another* was also The Writer.

The KITCO extracts on USAGOLD are titled "The Inside Story on the Gold-for-Oil Deal that could Rock the World's Financial Centers." As this remains the major compilation of *Another's* thoughts let us take a moment to consider its significance.

USAGOLD's introduction to the material suggests a very specific historical value the *Another's* postings: exposing the links in the oil-dollar-gold trade, a disclosure that could explain the major mystery of the day, i.e. the discovery of immense daily trading volumes on the London Bullion Market Association (LBMA) exchange. *Another* made a claim, noted the settlement venue for the oil-gold-dollar deals and Lo! The LBMA disclosed trading volumes that are astronomical.

This validation serves to give credence to other claims made by *Another* about the activities of "giants" with respect to gold; with respect to claims about off-market trading; and with respect to observations about global strategies and new developments (like the Euro).

But we don't need any validation of claims to get use of *Another's* views as thought experiments that can take us out of our blinkered world. In this crazy time of ours, we see investments as money, paper as value for the future, gold as a "barbaric relic," public trading venues as yielding price discovery, and currency values as the measure of all things.

Surely there is value in revisiting these assumptions.

Another's rich body of thought covers many aspects of gold, currency, finance, and the economy and in his day his readers focused on the topical matters of the Euro, the LBMA volumes, discovering the "true" price of gold, and the suppression of gold prices by the central banks and other actors. This last concern has remained a thread that connects his time to ours.

In July, 1997 the "Red Baron" began publishing a series of articles explaining the central banks' methods of gold price suppression. These articles, copyrighted to "Vronsky and Westerman," represent the tone of the times and a major concern of gold bugs and traders. They can be accessed here:

http://www.gold-eagle.com/research/redbaronndx.html

Articles of this quality show a maturity of thought that suggests a lot of good ideas were marinating a long time in the world of the late 1990s. *Another* contributed uniquely to this by giving us a motivation for central bank interventions - to keep cheap oil flowing by directing gold where it needed to go.

Today, we have the Gold Anti-Trust Action Committee (GATA), an active group with an interesting website:

http://www.gata.org/

GATA is building on the Red Baron/*Another* material in reportage and documentation. This often leads them into examining *agency*, the middlemen acting for central banks (or front running the central banks to make profits for their own accounts).

Although GATA's work complements this 1997 meme of price suppression, *Another*'s broader worldview is not much present, which is logical in that a committee formed for a specific purpose must comprise different people with different views working for a common outcome.

Soon after *Another's* retirement from the forum, his broader views found their home in in the emailings of someone calling himself "Friend of Another" (FOA).

FOA's messages to the USAGOLD mailing list are collected from February 2000. This compilation appears under the title "Walking the Gold Trail" at

http://www.usagold.com/goldtrail/archives/goldtrailone.html

FOA is interesting enough that his material is inevitably mentioned in the same breath as *Another's* and he deserves a book of his own. To the person considering reading FOA's large volume of writing, the best advice is to say, don't do it until you are reasonably familiar with *Another's*. Where Another's views were rooted in his personal and business associations and the operations which he observed or participated in, FOA's material seems to be pure analysis that uses *Another's* as its starting point. In other words, FOA builds upon "Thoughts!" and "Thoughts!" are the foundation for FOA's own, unique contributions. At times he elaborates ideas found in *Another*, but he is in no way a simple commentator on the body of "Thoughts!"

We find "Friend of Another" in September of 1998 writing to Michael Kosares, proprietor of USAGOLD.

> Michael, I'm looking for a large default in the paper gold market. With the major CB only buying now something is about to give as the most extended shorts can not cover. A default is most likely part of a game plan to get the ball rolling. This spike in gold will no doubt crush the dollar. The next few months will offer the last period of time to roll out of dollar assets at a good price. Of course, all of this is my opinion from and for the most part, *Another's*. (September 3, 1998)

To one steeped in the writings of *Another*, this is the opposite of "time will tell all things." Furthermore, adding *Another's* endorsement to your own views this way is obnoxious.

FOA's introductory posting to USAGOLD in 200 starts, "Hello everyone, I'm glad you could come along. My name is FOA."

In a later post he gave biographical information that suggests he was a small investor:

> I have made it clear that I follow in the footsteps of giants and by extension remain in *Another's* shadow. We have been buying gold all through the 90s as a portion of our savings. It's held just like any other currency and represents a major portion of the (my) pie. I also own some gold stocks (smile). But own them in a portion and for a reason that any leading gold mine executive can only crave: "they are held not for trading and in small enough portion that they will never be sold."

To the casual reader, it seems we have here a "small fry" capitalizing on the popularity of *Another* (who had stopped posting) to promote his own views. The tendency towards prediction is also annoying:

> The dollar faction is having a hard time keeping paper gold under $280. Now that the world has seen how the WA is placing Swiss Euro Gold, the paper markets should start to discount physical. I think weeks are all the time the dollar faction has left before things begin to change! (May 6, 2000)

But some of his predictions, taken out of the immediate, are precious. Here he is responding to a paper gold advocate:

> One day you will have a gold contract, the next it will be a currency contract. (May 25, 2000)

Twelve years later, future markets gave themselves permission to settle in cash rather than make physical deliveries.

The biggest idea FOA developed was "Freegold." Where *Another* saw the emergence of a gold or commodity backed currency, FOA imagined a world in which currencies and gold would trade in parallel. Gold would be allowed to find its level while currencies would find their level. To do this, one would need to break or at least revise the link to remove the incentive to manipulate gold prices.

"Freegold" is the touchstone of a prolific and intelligent blogger styling himself "Friend of a Friend of Another" (FOFOA). This nom de plume is homage to *Another* but moreso to FOA. FOFOA is committed to developing FOA's thought and he is well equipped intellectually and experientially to do so. A former trader, his posts are a rare mix of high reasoning, insight, and practical experience. He spends a lot of pixels on Freegold (and the Euro's potential role in that), but he does honor *Another* referring to root arguments. Here he has a nice quote from February 2013 that ties up *Another*, FOA and FOFOA into one neat package on the physical delivery of gold question:

> I don't expect anyone to intentionally break the system or "expose the fraud" [of paper markets] as you say. I don't think that was ever A/FOA's message. Those who dream of blowing up the system simply aren't capable of doing it, and those who are capable wouldn't dream of actually doing it.
>
> In your COMEX example you imagine someone trying to buy more of something than is obviously available at that time and then crying foul (or fraud) when the market can't deliver more than it has. Giants know that the best way to accumulate something at their level is slowly, over time, and within the volume offered on the market. And they also know what happens if they use their oversized weight to rock the boat:
>
>> *FOA: While so many of our gold bulls salivate at the prospects of some player calling for delivery and driving the gold derivatives market to the moon; it ain't gonna happen! Our world of dollar based gold derivatives has grown so large and become so integrated into supporting (hedging) international dollar assets, the central banks will band together to crush any delivery drive.*

That is a fine piece of *Another's* orthodoxy delivered by FOFOA using the pen of FOA. FOFOA frequently enters into dialog with readers and those readers may be up on their FOFOA but they are rarely familiar with *Another*, which causes painfully ignorant exchanges (on the reader side).

The quality of FOFOA's analysis has created a following large enough to provide him a living. See his work at

http://fofoa.blogspot.com/

A very popular website called Zero Hedge attracts an inordinate number of gold fans, silver bugs, and various traders. Zero Hedge is a news and commentary aggregator that interests itself especially in the corruption of regulated markets, the misdeeds from central banks, the folly of the European experiment, and government interventions of various sorts.

www.zerohedge.com

Zero Hedge operates inside some of the meme structures developed in the writings of *Another*. These include irregularities in gold leasing, encumbered assets of gold paper, price suppression, the grand strategies of central banking, currency wars, possession of physical, non-Western demand for physical, off-market transactions, the activity of "giants," the erosion of a dollar standard, etc.

These are not topics in any sense "owned" by *Another*, but his focus on them created a certain worldview and that is reflected in Zero Hedge's work, although the authors of Zero Hedge do not mention *Another* as an inspiration. This is a roundabout way of saying, those comfortable in the work of *Another* will get value from Zero Hedge.

On a side note, the Russian TV channel RT has delved deeply into the Zero Hedge talent pool for TV programming, tapping editors like Robert English, Bruce Krastins, and Michael Krieger for commentary. English has his own show ("Prime Interest") one episode of which was devoted to the Freegold concept.

Another anonymous blogger goes by "Victor the Cleaner" and as with FOFOA, he mixes a very high order of analytics with significant trading and institutional experience. "Victor" is an open disciple of *Another* who applies *Another's* thoughts to subjects that interest him. He reads FOFOA but is less under the influence of FOA than he is of *Another*. The material concerning Big Trader and The Writer were compiled by Victor for his blog. As superb as the thinking is, because of the time gaps between posts one can never be sure if this blog has died.

A final note: it would have been possible, in writing this book, to pepper it with quotes from these good people and from high profile gold advocates, to use those quotes to illustrate *Another's* points. This would have muddied the waters. Here, the reader can encounter *Another's* thoughts in small doses and simple form before going on to read "the real deal" complete and in the original.

Derivative material can come later.

FOA, FOFOA, and Victor represent a quality of analysis that will ensure *Another's* thought will have a future. This book does not rise to that level but is intended for a broader audience which appreciates a simpler introduction to these important views.

Appendix: Details of the Oil-Gold-Dollar Exchange

Another explained some technical aspects of the Gold-Oil-Dollar exchange. The blogger FOFOA's explanatory comments are worth including here as well and are marked.

Another (1/10/98):

> Question: What quantity of GOLD, paper or physical, has OIL traditionally purchased on an annual basis?
>
> Answer: From 1991, appx. 20m/oz./yr., now it is more.

FOFOA (2/27/13):

> ... 20 million ounces per year would have been about a third of annual global (not just Western) mining supply in 1991, all going to just one single player...

Another (10/18/97):

> A wise oil nation can strike a deal with the paper printers and in doing so come out on top. Go back a few years to the early 90s. Oil is very high, you offer to lower the US$ price in return for X amount of gold purchasing power. You don't care what the current commodity price of gold is, your future generations will keep it as real wealth to replace the oil that is lost. Before the future arrives gold will be, once again valued as money and can be truly counted on to appropriately represent all oil wealth!
>
> The Deal:
>
> We (an oil state) now value gold in trade far higher than currencies. We are willing to use gold as a partial payment for the future use of "all oil" and value it at $1,000 US. (only a small amount of oil is in this deal) And take a very small amount of gold out of circulation each month using its present commodity price. [...]
>
> Not all oil producers can take advantage of this deal as it is done "where noone can see". And, they know not what has happened for gold does not change in price! But I tell you, gold has been moved and its price has changed in terms of oil! For the monthly amount to be taken off the market has changed from $10 in gold (valued at $1,000) /per barrel to the current

$30 in gold /per barrel still valued at $1,000! Much of this gold was in the form of deals in London to launder its movement. Because of some Asians, these deals are no longer being rolled over as paper!

FOFOA (2/11/13):

First of all, they said they valued gold at $1,000/oz. in this deal and took $10 worth of physical off the market per barrel for a "small amount of oil." This was in the early days of the deal (c.1991). $10 is 1/100th of $1,000 so they were taking 1/100th of an ounce per barrel. In the early 90s the Saudis were producing about 9 million barrels per day. ANOTHER said that starting in 1991 they were taking about 20 million ounces of gold per year off the market through this deal. 20M ounces X 100 = 2 billion barrels of oil per year. Divide that by 365 days and it looks like the "small amount of oil in this deal" was 5.5M barrels per day, or about 61% of their production.

Another (10/5/97):

You see the trading medium changed. Oil went from $30++ to $19 + X amount of gold! Today it costs $19 + XXX amount of gold! Yes, gold has gone up and oil has stayed the same in most eyes. Now all govts. don't get gold for oil, just a few. That's all it takes. For now! When everyone that has exchanged gold for paper finds out its [gold's] real price in oil terms they will try to get it [gold] back.

In today's world of dark pools of capital and private stock exchanges (and secret stock dealing in major positions), it is much easier to believe in secret gold optionality on publicly priced oil.

The general public remains ignorant of private markets but they have been an established fact of life for many years. This kind of trading has certainly always been with us.

Made in the USA
Monee, IL
04 November 2026

67379300R00098